T.J. Schier & Sam Stanovich

Incentivize Solutions, Inc.

S.M.A.R.T. Restaurant Guide to Catering Domination
Copyright © 2020 T.J. Schier and Sam Stanovich

All rights reserved. Without limiting the rights under copyright reserved above, no part of this publication may be reproduced or transmitted in any form by any electronic or mechanical means (including photocopying, recording, or stored in or introduced into a retrieval system, or transmitted, in any form or by any means—except by a reviewer who may quote brief passages in a review to be printed in a magazine, newspaper, or on the Internet—without the prior written permission of the copyright owner.

The scanning, uploading, and distribution of this book via the Internet or via any other means without the permission of the publisher is illegal and punishable by law. Please purchase only authorized electronic editions and do not participate in or encourage electronic piracy of copyrightable materials. Your support of the author's rights is appreciated.

Although every effort to ensure the accuracy and completeness of information contained in this book, the author assumes no responsibility for errors, inaccuracies, omissions, or any inconsistency herein. Any slights of people, places, or organizations are unintentional.

Printed and bound in the United States of America.

ISBN 978-0-9716573-3-5

Book Design: FB Edit–Design

Published by Incentivize Solutions, Inc.

For more information on speaking inquiries and additional resources, visit **www.tjschier.com**.

CONTENTS

Preface	*v*
Introduction	*ix*
Part 1—Catering Overview	**1**
Chapter 1: Getting Started	3
Chapter 2: Catering Basics	16
Chapter 3: Financial Terminology	28
Part 2—Catering Pillars	**33**
Pillar 1: Team Member Buy-in	35
Pillar 2: Marketing	44
Pillar 3: Sales	58
Pillar 4: Operations	69
Pillar 5: Delivery & Pickup	76
Pillar 6: Follow-up	82
Part 3—Action	**87**
Chapter 4: Fishing in a Barrel Tactics	88
Chapter 5: Action Plan & Implementation	97

PREFACE

"There are two ways to do something: the right way, and again."
—Navy Seals

WANT MORE CATERING? Be careful what to wish for. Sam Stanovich and I have walked many catering (and operations) miles, each as a franchisee of a different sandwich chain, and look what it got us:

- 5,600 boxed meal order to feed an airline's employees at a large airport
- $100K in school catering in one year
- 38% catering sales annually (from a starting point of 3% annually)
- Traditionally slow business months, where overall sales increased 20% due to 60% of sales being catering

Not typical numbers from small sandwich shops but possible if one follows the systems described here to drive sales, introduce guests to the brand, and lead the charge to build revenue in the cut-throat catering business.

Think of us as your mentor, not just a coach. Coaches may or may not have "played the game". Sam and I have lived it for over a decade each. We tried and failed, adapted and succeeded, and have now put together a roadmap and tactical game plan for you to succeed.

Sam Stanovich, Firehouse Subs franchisee, and I have known each other since the year 2000 when he worked at the National Restaurant Association and I as a speaker and consultant. Fast forward 20 years when we both presented at a conference in early 2020 at a mutual friend's company, and the light bulb went off—the *Catering Domination* book. We both independently had catering success in our respective brands and put our heads together to create this guide to maximize catering business.

 Catering Domination

During the session, I was speaking on recruiting to the group of franchisees, and an analogy was used on how recruiting is like trying to catch a shark. One cannot find a shark in a lake—one must go to the right fishing spot (e.g., a vast ocean) with the right equipment and bait and get many hooks in the water. Once the shark bites, reel it in quickly to get it in the boat. Catering is no different.

The next day, Sam presented on his catering success and how the brand we were talking to could achieve the same level of success. He agreed catering was like fishing—but added one critical piece when he said, "I'd rather fish in a barrel versus fishing in an ocean." Prophetic. And the path to domination.

While the totality in size of catering is the size of an ocean, targeted efforts can narrow down where one looks for catering. What if one could learn how to fish in (the right) few small barrels, stocked with fish (catering leads) and had hooks in the water with the right bait? The restaurant could be FAR more successful and drive catering sales (and introduce more new guests to the brand to drive walk-in business). Hence, the book idea was born—put two catering heads together, teach what we know works, and provide resources and tactics to help grow catering sales for any restaurant.

A Little About T.J.

When my group first embarked on becoming a Which Wich franchisee in 2007, catering was not even part of the business plan. As the sandwich category became hypercompetitive, catering became a necessary means to survive. Since most of our locations were in large shopping centers in primarily residential areas, we didn't have traditional "catering" opportunities (e.g., for hospitals, pharmaceutical reps, and large offices).

Nevertheless, we found a unique niche that generated over a quarter million dollars in team and group meal catering across our locations annually, a huge marketing benefit by supporting the local community, a way to introduce the brand to thousands of students and their parents (getting paid for it) and creating a path to survive while many others failed.

PREFACE

When we started catering, we had no idea how to sell it. Trial by fire. For our group, schools were the low-hanging fruit. For others, it may be local offices, pharma reps, medical centers, or third-party delivery. Either way, catering has huge potential for many restaurants. Sam and I look forward to sharing battle-tested, effective ways to build business. Speaking of Sam, let's learn a bit more about his journey to catering domination.

A Little About Sam

The Firehouse Subs Stone Park (Illinois) launched November 2015. By February, winter had settled in, and the new unit opening honeymoon period had faded. At the time, sales seemed to be headed in the wrong direction. The location is not in a large power center but is located on a high traffic street with great density in the area. The site could be considered a C+. The brand was the driver. The main reason the guest visited the location was the awesome food and outstanding service, yet still sales were sliding. How many times has this scenario played out in restaurants across America?

As sales continued to slide, those traffic generators everyone looks for had to be found. Going after one guest at a time was difficult in the highly competitive sandwich and lunch space. Therefore, the catering market appeared to be a far more attractive (and speedy) solution to the sales challenges. As my wife says, "I'd rather be in a relationship and rich with 100 catering clients than to receive 1,000 one-time orders." But where does one begin since this book had not been written at that time?

Combining information gleaned from the best books (at the time) on the topic and reflecting back on experience in the hotel food and beverage business, a catering strategy was developed quickly. The vision was shared with the team. They were quickly trained, systems organized—and no looking back. Success did not come easy. Mistakes (trial and error) were made along the way, but the catering sales rose from a paltry 3% in 2016 to 22% in 2017. Wow!

Momentum (and reputation) built, and the sales mix grew to 34% catering

in 2018 and 38% in 2019. Sales in 2015 compared with sales in 2019 were up a staggering 60%—the majority of the increase due to catering—and much of the rest of the increase due to the many who were introduced to the brand through catering. In 2019, our restaurant delivered to 440 medical offices through pharma reps. With an average order size of $139, pharma reps generated over $60,000 in sales for one restaurant.

Catering has totally transformed the business model and added hundreds of thousands of dollars per year to the top—and the bottom line. What a tremendous feeling for the team when each week starts with a guaranteed base of business. The old thinking has been flipped now to "Live by catering and the gravy will be the walk-in business."

—*T.J. Schier*

INTRODUCTION

"Our mission is to feed our soldiers the best we can to ensure they are prepared to win and give the enemy their worst day."
—Chief Warrant Officer Five, Charles Hunter, U.S. Army Reserves

WHAT WAS I THINKING? My 1,600-square-foot sandwich restaurant (average sales of $12,000 per week) had just booked 4,400 boxed meals to be served over a five-day span to feed hungry high school band kids at back-to-back regional and state band contests. Producing $32,000 in catering in a small restaurant space while still operating and serving in-store guests—love that challenge!

Luckily, we had been serving this contest for a few years prior and had developed a stellar reputation for on-time delivery and high-quality organization, including labeling and grouping to ensure easy distribution and 100% accuracy. Band boosters and volunteers in charge of meals had been ordering from the restaurant year after year (and in various other locations throughout band season). They trusted us. However, we went from doing 2,800 boxes the year prior to an additional 50+% increase in the current year.

Our team was prepared as the GM and I spearheaded the effort. Those who wanted overtime were happily granted it during the week. With such a huge sales increase over the five days, labor costs would decrease significantly even with a little overtime. Most employees wanted extra hours to put aside a little extra cash for the upcoming holidays. We called in temps to fill in the rest of the needed workload to prep and prepare so many meals. When it was all over, 4,400 kids were fed (flawlessly albeit stressful at times). I'd worked 47 hours straight (never stayed up that long in my life before) and worked 107 total hours for the week. Crazy? Yes. Worth it? Yes.

 *Catering Domination*

Would you be worried if presented with that challenge? Not if one loves catering. Rise to the challenge and say "yes" first—then figure out how to execute it at a high level.

Welcome to the S.M.A.R.T. *Restaurant Guide to Catering Domination.* Whether new to catering or firmly entrenched in catering and hungry for more, it is time to get a larger slice of the huge catering pie. This book will be the roadmap to catering domination.

Why focus on catering? Seems like one more thing to worry about when running a restaurant. Often times, it's an entirely different business for the restaurant. Catering has often been referred to as the "13th month, 53rd week or 8th day." It's business with large order sizes, requires little extra labor, is consumed off premise (saving table space in the restaurant for others), and frequently introduces guests to the brand in the best way possible—by tasting the food.

Catering comes in all shapes and sizes such as entrees, packaged deals, boxed meals, sides, small groups, large company events, and so on. To get the most out of this book, pick the points that will work in the business area around the restaurant. Also, however, get outside the comfort zone and try new tactics or things attempted without this knowledge and failed in the past. If there is no advertising promoting catering or someone out "beating the streets," then how will sales increase? After all, the fish don't just jump in the boat.

Listen, we were once in the same boat once and heard all the excuses: "Our food isn't as good when catered"; "Catering has such high food and paper costs"; "I have no control over it once it leaves"; "Shouldn't have to do catering just to survive"; "Our brand should advertise it"; or "I don't even know where to begin to market our catering." Sit there, complain, and be passed by or get smart and dominate the catering market in your area.

Financially, while it may increase the cost percentages, it raises overall profitability. There are not too many ideas out there to generate thousands of dollars in PROFIT to the restaurant. The $32,000 we had in catering sales made over $12,000 in profit over a five-day period. Compared with

INTRODUCTION

doing $12,000 per week in sales, it takes a couple months to earn $12,000 in profit (and is a lot more work). Depth over width. Interested now?

Booking $10,000 in football team meals over 10 weeks delivering at 3 p.m. in the afternoon not only generates about $5,000 in profit over that time and puts the brand in front of targeted and potential guests, it also engages the brand into the community. Providing catering lunch to a car dealer, hospital, doctor's office, teacher's in-service day or catering events, such as a wedding, family reunion, tailgate, or special day in someone's, life drives simple profitable sales for the restaurant.

Just as joining a gym does not guarantee physical transformation, putting in the right work does. Simply reading this book, hoping catering clients call or griping about how competitive the business is will not transform sales. Putting in the right work will. Think of this guide as a personal catering trainer—providing the right "exercises" to do to transform sales. Then, it's up to the reader to do the exercises and reap the rewards. We are your trainers and coaches—showing what has worked, the results to be achieved, which exercises to do, and what things to avoid. Domination is the goal.

Restaurant owners, operators, and managers in full-service, casual dining, quick-service, fast casual, or food trucks can create a catering arm of their business to drive incremental revenue (often with large check averages). We both started small but quickly found a catering niche (albeit different ones) to build revenue and market the brand through catering.

The catering journey is not one to take lightly nor tried solo—neither of our groups did. I would like to personally thank everyone who helped at S.M.A.R.T. Restaurant Group over the years to become a beacon of catering success. The managers and team members who executed at a high level were the ones who truly are the catering superstars. Anyone can sell catering, but catering rock stars are needed to turn it into reality for the clients and guests.

Sam and I would also like to thank pioneers in this field who enlightened operators to marketing tips, software to better systematize catering, and some out-of-the-box thinking on what is possible around catering sales and

 *Catering Domination*

execution: Steve Bigari from Synq3 Solutions, Erle Dardick and his team, founder of Monkey Media Software, and Michael Attias, founder of Cater Zen.

This book is a pillar book in the *S.M.A.R.T. Restaurant Guide* series. The foundation book, *S.M.A.R.T. Restaurant Guide to Effective Food Service Operations*, outlines the overarching tactics and strategies to build a business that out-executes the competition. The recruiting book, along with this catering book, are pillars in helping create *THE* restaurant, and caterer, of choice. Time to go fishing (in a barrel) for catering domination.

As you read through and see mentions of forms and examples, note that they are housed online at www.cateringdomination.com. The site includes resources, webinars, recommendations, and an option for mentoring you through the journey to Catering Domination!

HAPPY CATERING!

PART 1

Catering Overview

CHAPTER 1
Getting Started

"If you're offered a seat on a rocket ship, don't ask what seat! Just get on."
—Sheryl Sandberg

AS MENTIONED EARLIER, great catering companies focus their efforts on fishing in a barrel (many barrels). To be effective, great fishermen know what they want to catch, which tools and resources they need, where their competitors are fishing, and, once they get to their fishing hole, they throw several hooks with the right bait into the water.

You may be thinking, "I can't sell catering" or "it's too much work" or "I hate to sell". All emotions we both felt many times. We wasted money trying too many things that did not work. We uncovered some hidden gems. We struggled. We learned how to deal with rejection and keep pushing toward success. We wish we had this information before we started. Since we love helping other restaurant owners and managers, that work we put in was for your benefit as well. You can have the same (or greater) success.

To move catering forward in the restaurant, there are a few key steps to follow:

- Define your business
- Catering vision and goal
- Assess operations
- Delivery
- Menu
- Competition
- Budgeting
- Training

SMART RESTAURANT GUIDE TO *Catering Domination*

Define Your Business

Similar to losing weight, getting in shape, or improving finances, the current landscape must be understood to move the needle. Defining the business in terms of catering impact is the first step in improving catering sales. Start with the following diagnostics:

Sales
(Not all will apply to every restaurant; total should add up to 100%.)

Dine-in	_____%
Take-out	_____%
Third-party	_____%
Delivery (in-house)	_____%
Catering	_____%

Per-Person Average (PPA)

Breakfast	$_____
Lunch	$_____
Dinner	$_____

Marketing spend for catering advertising: _____

TOP-5 CATERING ITEMS AND PROFIT MARGIN	
ITEM	MARGIN
1.	
2.	
3.	
4.	
5.	

Average catering order size: $ _____

What catering sales level is envisioned (realistically but a stretch)? If the restaurant is part of a chain or a franchise, how does this location compare

GETTING STARTED

with the system averages and the leading locations in the area of catering sales?

To help build the business, one needs clarity on the vision and goals for the restaurant(s). Own the community. Be the "mayor of the mile". Guests should know the manager or owner of the restaurant and what he or she stands for. Fast-casual and quick-service restaurants need to own the area within a 5- to 7-minute drive, while full-service restaurants pull from a larger radius.

Vision and Goal

Vision Statement (definition)

An aspirational description of what an organization would like to achieve or accomplish in the midterm or long-term future. It is intended to serve as a clear guide for choosing current and future courses of action.

Specific to catering, put together a vision statement and goal. For example:

In the 12 months, we will dominate our competition by providing the most craveable catering options; accurate, timely execution; and exemplary service resulting in an increase of 10% in catering sales. Within three years, catering will generate 20% of total sales and be over $200,000 in revenue.

This statement must be shared with the team. Have the team help create it and take the opportunity to teach the importance of catering sales and how it will benefit everyone. Additional sales mean more hours for everyone and a much healthier business. If it is not a shared vision, how can the teams rally to help? Catering is NOT a one-person business: It takes the entire team for its successful execution. When the team knows the vision, understands why and their role, and has an interest in the outcome, everyone, including management, is accountable to achieving the vision and goal.

NOTE: Restaurants that are part of a franchise or brand may have territorial limits or boundaries. In those cases, there may be less ponds to fish in, but there are still plenty of good places to try. Determining and properly scaling the minimum order and distance are key to success. Remember

 Catering Domination

these are guidelines. If sales are slow, one can provide value to the guest by waiving a delivery fee or order minimum. But when the business ramps up, having a solid foundation of catering adds value, sales, and profits to the restaurant.

Assess Operations and Capabilities

As catering goals are set and shared, and the tactics and strategies to achieve the goals are materializing, ensure an honest assessment of operations and its capabilities is completed. For example, what is the largest order that can be produced currently due to staffing, facility, and production capabilities?

If a 1,000 boxed lunch order is received, is there enough room to purchase, produce, store, and properly deliver to the guest? Examine the facility and operations to understand what guardrails need to be placed on catering. Get creative if needed. Adding capacity may be difficult, but renting a storage trailer or hiring temps for a large order can certainly be justified financially.

Many restaurants may not have enough refrigeration or cold storage for additional items needed when catering volume increases. Adding shelving or rearranging dry storage may be required to have ample room for organization of catering and packaging supplies. If the catering provided involves production and delivery of hot food, are there enough holding cabinets? For delivery (if being done in-house), are there enough insulated delivery bags or boxes (Cambro Go Boxes, for example)?

As catering sales grow, be prepared (in advance) with solutions for additional equipment needs, off-site storage (if required), and staffing plans so catering orders do not have to be turned away. As mentioned earlier, catering is a different business. Most likely, the restaurant was not designed for 20%–40% of the sales being catering orders, so adjustments must be made to the facility and organization.

A few other potential needs to consider:
- Will wheeled carts be needed to ease the delivery process?
- What proper vehicles and insurance is needed if doing deliveries?

GETTING STARTED

- Who will be the point person overseeing catering marketing, sales, and production?
- What supplies are needed for proper (branded) catering presentation?

A great catering manager once said, "Do not size the need for what you have today, size for the business you want."

Delivery

For many companies, delivery is done by the restaurant's employees. Others utilize a third-party delivery service. When considering taking delivery in-house, there are numerous costs to consider beyond just hiring delivery drivers. A few items to examine:

- Additional insurance needs due to providing delivery
- Driving record and background checks completed on drivers
- Mileage allowances and travel costs system
- Delivery driver's responsibilities when no deliveries are needed

The benefit to in-house delivery is controlling the entire catering experience through the delivery and setup process. An employee of the restaurant is interacting with the guest, not a third-party contractor.

Many restaurants have a designated person to take larger catering deliveries ordered in advance and outsource short-notice deliveries or ones requested during peak restaurant times to third-party services. Third-party services price their fees based on order size and distance, so ensure those costs are built into the pricing quoted to the client. Do the homework and make the right decision for the restaurant and its guests (both dine-in and catering).

Delivery Fees

Many restaurant owners and managers worry about the cost of delivery being too high in the eyes of the catering buyer. Get over that hesitation. Many catering buyers are spending their company's money and are not concerned about the delivery fee. They pay for TRUST. Is the restaurant delivery trustworthy and reliable (i.e., being on time, 100% accurate, and

 Catering Domination

friendly service at pickup, drop-off, and when setting up)? If so, the catering client will pay. Catering order sizes typically average $150–$200, so a fee of $25 (usually of a company's money) is generally not a deal breaker to the client.

Delivery Fees (Internal)
Here is an example of how delivery fees (without being too expensive) can be set when the restaurant is providing the delivery service so potential catering guests are not turned away. While your restaurant may not deliver this far, a fee structure such as this one balances the costs to cover the delivery (labor, mileage, time) with the size and cost of the delivery to the client.

Delivery Fee	Order Minimum	Delivery Radius
$0	$35	5 miles
$10	$35	10 miles
$15	$75	15 miles
$25	$125	20 miles
$35	$200	25 miles
$40	$200	30+ miles

Delivery Fees (Third-Party Services)
As mentioned earlier, delivery fees charged by third-party services are based on time and distance. Talk to approved delivery companies utilized to obtain their cost structure. The internal fee structure previously mentioned is modeled after typical fees charged by these companies. Therefore, posted delivery pricing online (or quoted over the phone) can be the same whether the restaurant or a third-party company delivers.

The Catering Menu
Many readers will not be allowed to have input on the catering menu, as it has been set up by the corporation, franchisor, or ownership. If so, review

GETTING STARTED

the product mix to understand what current catering clients are buying. The key is to suggest what is popular with what is profitable. If there is decision-making ability for the catering menu, in most restaurants, look at what sells. Catering is different! A Mediterranean concept may only sell kabobs to 2% of dine-in guests but five times as many buy that item as a catering option. What sells in the restaurant is not always what sells outside the restaurant! Look at the product mix and evolve the menu to better adapt to current trends and competition and remove slower moving options.

When reviewing the product mix and what to promote, a few keys to consider:

- **Hook:** What is the one hook that always lands the fish? Highlight that item or package on the menu. Lead with the signature and most-popular catering items or packages when talking with potential buyers.
- **Simplicity:** Is the catering menu simple in the eyes of the client? Many buyers do not want to have to calculate pricing of individual items or navigate through lengthy, hard-to-understand menus. Encourage package deals when possible (i.e., sandwich, chips, sweets, and dessert or entrée, two sides, beverage and dessert) for a set price per person.
- **Batch Production:** Catering sales can be maximized by being able to batch produce items. BBQ, tacos or fajitas, bulk sales, pasta and sides are all examples of simple-to-produce items in large quantities. Boxed (or bagged) lunches, individual plates and custom packages are more difficult to produce and put a cap on catering due to lengthy production times.
- **Pricing:** How does pricing compare to clients' budgets? Many make a purchase on a per-person budget of $8.95 or $11.95 per person and so on. Are there competitive package deals to be packaged and highlighted on the menu and online to make purchasing "one-click"?
- **Top Sellers:** Look at the top-selling catering items. Make adjustments on those items as needed as those items drive catering profitability. How does your price compare to competitors? Offerings? If you sell a BBQ platter and it's $7.95 per person, including iced tea, yet your competitor is charging $8.95 per person plus drinks, are you leaving

 *Catering Domination*

money on the table? Yes, one could argue you are winning on price. And, you may be so busy with catering, you feel it is priced right. However, imagine if you raised the price $1 to be competitive (but are still providing better value as the tea is included), selling 500 per week would net out $500 additional sales (and about $480 additional profit dollars if you are not franchised and paying royalties on the additional sales). Be competitive and provide more value—the guest will pay for it! Priced too cheaply and money is left on the table. Not priced competitively, and sales will be lost to the competition.

Worried about pricing and the menu? Here's a success story:

Our team lunch box program as $6 per box for ten years. We were always hesitant to raise the price. The bottom line? We are BETTER than anyone priced cheaper than us ... and CHEAPER than anyone better than us. We added a second-sized sandwich option ($9 per box) to provide something the competition did not to build sales yet stay price competitive. In 2019, we finally raised the boxed lunch prices for teams to $7 and $10 for the two sandwich-sized boxed lunches. Only only one school was lost due to price. Two others we had to make a donation to the booster clubs for $250 each to offset the increase. Net-net, we sold over 15,000 boxed meals at the higher price of $1 per box, generating a healthly sales increase for the business with a minimal expense.

Great fishermen chum the waters—in other words, they throw chopped-up fish over the side of the boat to attract the fish they want to catch. The catering menu is like chum—it is used to attract catering buyers. Ensure it is simple and highlights packaged deals for easy purchase decisions. Finally, narrow down the offerings: Keep the items on-brand and eliminate high-cost, low-selling items, as those items muddy the purchasing decision for the buyer. Leverage the competitive advantage of the signature items to ensure a craveable, profitable menu (i.e., items that catering guests will try at the event and then have to visit the restaurant to try out).

The Competition

Great fishermen know who they are competing against to hook that prized catch. Does the restaurant know who the competitors are? Ask catering

GETTING STARTED

buyers to list what companies they buy from. Is the restaurant mentioned? If a catering buyer is pitched and the order lost to a competitor, ask who got the order and why they were chosen.

Too often, managers are in the dark regarding catering competition. In the sandwich segment alone, there are a dozen or so national chains, regional chains, and countless independent sandwich shops that cater. If the catering buyer wants sandwiches, the marketplace is already crowded. Catering buyers, however, are often not only deciding which company but also what type of food: BBQ, chicken, pizza, Mexican, Asian, Mediterranean, Italian, vegan, sandwich, and many other styles could be desired. As caterers, the competition is all segments.

Search the competitors' catering websites and brochures. When making deliveries, look for other companies' information or logoed cups, plates, or napkins in the area setting up. The competitors are right there. Another reconnaissance tip for scouting out the competition is to review services such as EZ Cater. Enter the restaurant address and see what restaurants show up at the top of the list—in all segments.

Once the competition has been defined, place orders. Call that restaurant and receive the entire experience. What is it doing well? Ideally, deliver to the house or spouse's office versus the restaurant but do not be shy. Heck, order to have it delivered to the restaurant. Everyone is as sick of their own food as is the next restaurant. If questioned, say the team is being rewarded today by getting lunch or dinner catered in.

COMPETITION CATERING SHEET EXAMPLE	
CATERING PER PERSON COST	
Breakfast	$
Lunch	$
Dinner	$

Catering Domination

TOP-5 CATERING ITEMS AND COST	
ITEM	COST
1.	
2.	
3.	
4.	
5.	

ONLINE REVIEWS

CATERING WEBSITE FEEDBACK

SOCIAL PRESENCE FOR CATERING ON INSTAGRAM, FACEBOOK, LINKEDIN, EZ CATER, ETC.

GETTING STARTED

Experiencing the top-five competitors will help focus on their service, quality, delivery, and follow-up. Actual data and experiencing and tasting the competition shows the reality and lets everyone know how high the competitive bar is to beat. The sooner one understands who the popular competitors are in the market, the sooner changes can be made to build catering sales.

Budget

The next step toward catering domination is building a budget. After evaluating the business and competition, list out the items needed to be competitive to best position the restaurant to build catering sales. Expenses could include:

- Catering equipment (carts, insulated bags or boxes, new packaging, etc.)
- Restaurant modifications (storage, equipment, etc.)
- Catering menu design and printing
- Marketing expenses: digital ads, website updates
- Labor expenses: catering sales manager, labor for feet on the street, delivery drivers
- POS/software expense: catering CRM and any POS upgrades needed (if any)

Preparing a catering budget, with a separate line (or lines) on the P&L, will help the restaurant maintain cost controls and help one better understand what is driving the sales and generating the return on investment. One likely will not undertake all these expenses at one time, but preparing a budget to understand what expenses could be incurred will allow for far more accurate planning.

For example, the catering software may not be purchased until catering sales exceed a set hurdle per month. Labor will be allocated weekly to do "feet-on-the-street" initially, but the catering sales manager will not be added until catering sales exceed a set hurdle per month as well. Repeat the process for any restaurant modifications or other large expenses and work toward domination.

 *Catering Domination*

Training

No different than any other aspect of a restaurant, if one wants outstanding performance, training needs to be thorough, detailed, and excellent. Much of what needs to be trained for catering orders is not part of any position's initial training. Producing the food for the order is the simplest part and likely the part where the employee is most comfortable. However, there are far more training topics to be covered:

- Prospecting script
- Taking the order
- Order entry
- Order production
- Checking the order for pickup/delivery
- Releasing the order for delivery
- Delivery and setup
- Order follow-up

For each topic, expectations must be defined in the training. Poor, incomplete, or no training on the prospecting or order taking will eliminate the opportunity for a restaurant to maintain a catering business. Poor, incomplete, or no training on order production and checking the order? Mistakes will happen, and the restaurant will never provide catering for that guest again.

Document the necessary steps in each section of the above topics. Where applicable, use photos with text boxes (or make short videos using smartphone), as they are far more effective to train an employee instead of long pages of text. Have the employees review the applicable sections and then roleplay scenarios for:

- Prospecting
- Order taking
- Delivery and setup standards
- Order follow-up

For the actual production, the best training is hands-on (after reviewing

GETTING STARTED

the print materials). Make each one of the catering items the restaurant sells—perhaps one to three items per day so the employees can practice production. Next, use the pickup/delivery checklist to double-check the order and roleplay the pickup or release for delivery process. Next, deliver the order to a lucky local business (let the business know it is the "business of the day" and provide catering menus and bounce-back coupons).

Remember once the food is prepared and leaves the restaurant, it is the moment of truth. Is there 100% certainty on the food quality, accuracy (including all sides, condiments, utensils, and plateware), and timeliness? If the team was trained properly and utilizes the systems in place, then, yes, there is 100% certainty.

CHAPTER ACTION ITEMS

➢ *Review financial terminology to ensure understanding by entire management/ownership team*

➢ *Define your vision and goals for catering*

➢ *Assess operations and determine needs*

➢ *Review catering menu offerings (if you have the ability to change it)*

➢ *Scout the competition!*

➢ *Set/edit delivery fee structures to cover delivery costs*

➢ *Train staff on catering menu*

CHAPTER 2
Catering Basics

"You don't have to be good to start ... you just have to start to be good!"
—Joe Sabah

THE IMPORTANCE OF CATERING to most restaurants sales has been established and some numbers shared. The numbers are already impressive. Realize, however, the magnitude of just how big the catering opportunity is in the marketplace.

2020 State of the Industry

There are over 1 million restaurant locations in the United States, employing over 15.5 million workers. Projections for 2020 sales are over $800 billion (pre-COVID-19 pandemic); 2030 estimate industry sales at over $1.2 trillion. Catering sales in 2020 are projected to be $40 billion of the total industry sales (4.5%). Catering sales are comprised of $25 billion in business-to-consumer (B2C) and $15 billion business-to-business (B2B). Shocked B2C is higher? There is a $40 billion pie out there. Who wants a slice?

According to the National Restaurant Association State of the Industry 2020, the majority of full-service operators and over two-thirds of fast casual operators offer catering. Among those restaurants that do cater, 90% report their catering sales rose or stayed the same during the last two years. Meaning less than 1 in 10 operators reported a decline in their catering sales. Catering sales are on the rise.

Before fishing for catering sales, there is need to understand the basic terminology, tools, and jargon—and how to effectively use that knowledge to help convince any skeptics. A foundational understanding of the catering landscape is needed. Choose the areas to focus on. Learn how to fish in

CATERING BASICS

one barrel (as my company did with schools), perfect the sales and systems, then fish in more barrels. After all, it's easier to fish in a few barrels to catch a few types of fish (catering clients) versus trying to catch anything out in the vast ocean. Targeted fishing in barrels saves time, energy, and expense, and maximizes the payoff.

There may be familiarity with some or much of this jargon. If so, take this opportunity to teach it to others. Everyone working in the restaurant must be focused on identifying catering opportunities by engaging with guests. Selling catering must become a cultural part of the business—not a program. EVERY guest is an opportunity—simply teach the team to see beyond the guest as a transaction today. Guests are the easiest option to begin generating catering sales—they already love the brand and food. Doing a little recon or undercover work allows one to best serve their needs beyond their meal today.

Talk to them, find out where they work, how often they order catering (or who the catering contact is at their company), if they have kids in middle or high school on a team or in a group that might need food, and so on. EVERY guest is an opportunity. As hospitality legend Danny Meyer of Union Square Hospitality Group says, "ABCD—Always Be Connecting Dots." To connect the dots, one has to know and speak the lingo.

Catering Basics

Catering vs. Group Ordering

There may not be a difference in our world between "catering" and "group ordering" (both are consumed off-premise), but there is on the guest side. "Catering" means "company pays" while "group ordering" in most cases means "pay for our own." Why is this distinction important? Simple. When contacting a company, church, or school and asking, "Does the company cater?" they often say "No" as their company does not pay for people's meals. However, if the question is changed to, "Does the office ever order lunch out or group order?" they often say "Yes."

That's the signal to present what options are available. Perhaps they order online from the regular menu or set up catering options such as

 Catering Domination

boxed meals, even though everyone is paying individually. Ultimately, group ordering and catering are eaten away from the restaurant. Think of it as "outside sales." Either way, both should be a focus and require slightly different approaches. Yes, it is semantics, but it makes a big difference in the outcome of the questions asked—guide the guest to "yes" by asking questions in the most effective way.

Guest Terminology

While guests consume catering offsite, hospitality still needs to be delivered both in the care when making the food as well as the pickup or delivery experience. "Philoxenia" is a Greek word meaning "friend to the stranger." In ancient Greek virtues, there was great respect and honor bestowed from host to guest. Therefore, hosts are dutifully bound to offer hospitality, food, and drink to anyone (even when catering).

Catering

Catering is typically a preset or separate menu from the main restaurant menu. The company (or a vendor or client) usually pays for catering to a business. Based on the typical catering menu offerings, it might be boxed or bundled meals, sandwich trays, bulk proteins, and sides or a "build your own" such as a burger, sandwich, taco, or fajita bar. Many people personally cater events as well, so do not limit catering only to businesses.

Often the catering decision (and ideal product[s] they need) are driven by how the group is going to be eating. Clarifying questions will help guide the guest to his/her ideal catering order. How many people? Budget? How will the food be served? Is it a buffet, plated or grab-n-go meal? Buffet style? If so, bulk portions or sandwich trays where their guests build their own meals may be the best way to go.

Is it a quick meal or eating on the go such as a team meal or a working lunch? A boxed lunch may make more sense as the box has all items (e.g., a sandwich, chips, fruit, dessert, condiments, and utensils) in the box for easy transport and consumption. If talking to the guest in-store or on the phone, find out this critical information to provide the best catering options to them.

CATERING BASICS

Group Ordering

"Group ordering" means the guest is typically ordering off the regular menu for a group of people, and usually each is paying for their own. Delivery is often required (or done via third-party delivery company). Orders could be called-in (right in the middle of the rush, of course), placed online, e-mailed, and ... *gasp* ... faxed to the location.

While it may be "catering" to us internally, it's different in the eyes of the guest. Either way, we need to ensure 100% accuracy and timeliness. As the result of flawless execution, the buyer or admin who selected the restaurant for the meal will build trust (and earn kudos from co-workers). These orders are to be treated like a catering order: double-check the order for 100% accuracy, ensure all side items are with the order, and offer assistance to the car if needed (or set up inside if a delivery).

With the continued rise of takeout, delivery, curbside and guests dining away from the restaurant, group ordering will be a larger percentage of restaurant revenue and an opportunity for those on the forefront.

Business-to-consumer (B2C) is a huge revenue stream whether "catering" or "group ordering". Educate guests on the offerings the restaurant provides, especially "meal kits", bulk offerings and "party platters" as these items are quite easy to produce for the restaurant, have a high ticket average, and a strong perceived value by the consumer.

Ordering Methods

Catering (and group) orders are typically placed:
- Online
- Phone
- In person
- Fax (really?)
- Third-party catering site such as companies like EZ Cater or GrubHub Catering.

Either way, all order information needs to be gathered; for example, order details, type of catering (pickup, drop-off, full-service—more on those

 Catering Domination

shortly), food allergies or special requests, contact person and phone/email, time needed, and payment.

Many of the competitors ignore the phone ("we are too busy"), or the restaurant rushes callers through the order process to get back to the in-store business. Huge sales opportunities are lost. It is a challenge to serve in-store guests and call-in orders, especially with their large order size and high expectations. One never knows who could be on the other end of that call (hint: it is MONEY), so answer the phone and provide stellar service.

Payments

Payments may be made a variety of ways. Ensure the team is aware of the procedures on payment processing as catering demands a variety of options:

- **At the time of order (online or called-in):** Ideally, ring up the day of the order so the sales match the usage for that day. If the guest wants it rung up at the time of the order, ring up and attach receipt to the order details to ensure the person working the day of the order is aware it has been paid.
- **At the time of pickup or delivery:** Guests may call in the day of the order to pay, pay when they pick it up, or process a payment with a mobile payment processor or tablet at the delivery location (if the restaurant has one).
- **At a later date (aka "house account", meaning the restaurant extends credit terms to the company or group):** The sale is entered the day of the order, but the payment is made at a later date (tendered to the house account on the day of the order for that company). Many companies require house accounts so if they are not currently offered, get it set up.
- **Pre-paid:** Some groups, such as school sports teams (or the parents), prepay for their entire season's worth of meals. A house account is created for that group, and the amount received is entered into that account. A declining balance will be used. Sales are entered on the day they occur and posted to that respective house account, which will bring that account eventually to zero.

Payments can be a touchy subject that many restaurant owners fret over,

CATERING BASICS

primarily "house accounts". The restaurant must have a defined (and utilized) process for:
- How customers are granted credit terms. Application process?
- Maximum amount of credit?
- Payment terms (7, 14, or 30 days)?
- Interest rate charged on late accounts?
- How late accounts will be contacted and collected.

Late payments are a touchy subject. Often, large corporations are quite slow to pay vendors, especially small ones like restaurants. This delay puts the restaurant in a cash flow crunch. Trying to collect is both time consuming and frustrating as the restaurant does not want to alienate the client while trying to collect monies owed. Balancing the long-term value of the catering client with the short-term cash flow needs of the business is a challenge.

Types of Catering

There are three primary types of catering orders: pickup, drop-off, and full-service. Restaurants may or may not offer all these types of catering. Let's take a closer look at each:

Pickup Catering

As the name suggests, guests can "pick up" (or bring it to them curbside) their catering from the location. This type of catering order is the simplest, as it does not require delivery, just production, assembly, and bagging to have it ready at the stated time. Once the guest arrives to pick up the order, double-check the order with the guest to ensure it is 100% accurate and includes all side items, special requests, condiments, plateware (if needed), beverages, cups, and utensils (if applicable). Offer to assist the guest to his/her vehicle and ensure the packaging is sealed tight and organized for *easy* transport into the guest's event, as someone from the restaurant will not be there to help the person unload and set up.

 Catering Domination

Drop-Off Catering

The majority of catering ordered is "drop-off" catering—the order is dropped off at the designated location such as an office, venue, meeting room, school, home, or the like. Depending on the restaurant's policies, someone from the team may make the delivery, or it may be done by a third-party delivery service. Either way, it is crucial to have a checklist to ensure all items and utensils are with the order prior to it leaving the restaurant. Drop-off can be a bit misleading as the majority of the time it isn't just "dropped off." Many guests or clients need the order set up in the designated location at the delivery site such as a breakroom, meeting room, or cafeteria.

Having catering setup standards is critical. Modify as needed for the guest or client. Once done setting up, double-check with the guest to ensure it is set up to their liking. Take a photo of the setup in case to help alleviate issues as well as to send to the restaurant manager to note delivery time and setup was done 100% correctly. The photo could also be sent to a client who is not on site such as a pharma rep who ordered catering for a doctor's office.

Full-Service Catering

This type of catering is more elaborate as the restaurant (or catering company) is providing a staff on-site to serve the catering. Full-service catering typically involves facility setup, staffing of banquet servers, station attendants, bartenders, and working with additional third-party vendors such as music and video. While some restaurants will set up buffets and have serving attendants, much of the full-service catering business is handled by event companies, professional catering companies, and large venues. Also, since there has been much written on this topic, we will not focus on this type of catering in the book.

Third-Party Services

Most restaurant operators love to run restaurants and hate to deal with many

CATERING BASICS

of the newer, ancillary items such as point of sale (POS), software, delivery, marketing, and so on. Therefore, it is prudent in many cases to partner with others (aka "third parties") to outsource some of the headaches to experts in those areas. These services have a cost. Analyze if the benefit justifies the cost for the brand.

Third-Party Ordering Sites

Third-party catering ordering sites are increasing in popularity. Restaurants pay a commission to the third-party ordering site for marketing services and getting the order for the restaurant. While operators and owners would all love for the catering guests to order directly from their own company's website, many guests order from these third-party sites. Why?

- The guest can order from multiple vendors at once such as a BBQ bundle from Company A and desserts from Company B).
- The guest can save favorite orders and easily reorder.
- Familiarity with the third-party site versus having to learn each restaurant's ordering nuances (and having to have multiple apps or website accounts to place catering orders).
- Some of these sites offer perks such as gift cards to those placing the orders to build their loyalty.
- Many companies only allow one food vendor setup in their accounting system to issue payments. Those placing orders utilize a third-part site, so they can order from countless vendors yet still comply with their company restrictions of only one food vendor.

Complain all one wants regarding the fees these companies charge but realize that catering clients will still use the sites as it is easy for *them*. Additionally, it introduces competitors to your buyer. Plus, receiving 70%–80% of the price of a catering sale (after paying commission) is better than 100% of no sale. Also realize, these companies often pay weekly or bi-weekly, causing a delay in the cash flow of the restaurant. More on how to maximize sales and profitability of this ordering option later in the book.

 Catering Domination

Third-Party Delivery Services

For most operators, delivery is a dichotomy. While the restaurant wants to keep control of the food through the delivery process, the sporadic nature of catering orders creates scheduling headaches for restaurants. Also, delivery is entirely different business. It usually requires additional insurance to cover drivers and, overall, is a headache many operators do not want to handle. Therefore, third-party delivery services have popped up. Operators can choose from any number of delivery companies. Since the space is fluid and ever-changing, the companies are not listed here as they frequently change or consolidate.

Some restaurant companies use courier services who deliver everything from food to packages or documents for businesses. Others use third-party delivery services focused on food delivery. While the fees these companies charge are relatively steep, there are two advantages to use third-party delivery services:

- Delivery fees are often passed onto the client so the net cost to the restaurant is minimal at worse
- Restaurants can focus on their expertise—making amazing food by not having to deal with another part of the business

There are some drawbacks when using third-party delivery services.

- Most importantly, the restaurant loses control over not just food quality, but also, the service experience as the driver is contracted out and is not an employee of the brand
- Fees charged are often quite high. Yes, you can charge the fee back to the client (letting them know in advance

When selecting a delivery partner, ensure the company is reputable, has the proper insurance and coverage, and shares a common culture of a high level of service. After all, if the driver is late, sloppy, or does not provide the proper level of setup and service at the delivery point, YOU will be the guilty party in the eyes of the guest and lose future business. Meet with the delivery company, look at its online reviews, ask for references, and, finally, provide specific standards of service and setup the restaurant has, so it can be provided to the driver to ensure guests receive the experience they deserve.

Focus on controlling your delivery process. Yes, you will have to consider mileage and wear and tear on the delivery vehicle but, ultimately, ensuring a high-quality dining expericence will help.

Other Third-Party Services

There are a few other third-party services to consider including:
- Outsourced call center to handle all catering orders as well as answering the calls for takeout and delivery
- Street Teams—a number of marketing teams can be hired to canvas the area or cold call names/companies on the list they are provided

Decisions such as these can be made via a simple analysis to determine if the path is right for you.

Catering Software

Once the restaurant has built catering momentum, it often makes sense to invest in catering software to help automate processes, assist operations, and minimize mistakes. One can do many of these processes manually or in a spreadsheet for free. Based on the catering volume and how taxing it is on operations, the determination can be made on whether or not to invest in it.

The key components and benefits of the catering software reviewed are:
- **CRM (Customer Relationship Manager):** This assists in tracking the prospects list (who, segment, type and communication history, and follow-up), customer list, and purchase history, ability to segment buyers by industry type and email and SMS (text) marketing capability. It also helps track additional communications such as phone calls, emails, thank you letters, and follow-up.
- **Proposals, Ordering, Invoicing:** Many customers require a formal proposal and itemized cost to obtain approval prior to ordering. Providing professional proposals or quotes from the software is a nice benefit and is necessary in many cases. Once approval has been received, the proposal information becomes the order details.

 *Catering Domination*

The system can also generate invoices to be emailed and presented at pickup or delivery. Far too often, a guest loses the POS receipt, the driver forgets to bring it, or the driver leaves it on the dashboard and the sun ruins the receipt. Having a professional proposal and invoicing system closes the deal for many customers.

If the business cannot be A+ in the eyes of the customer BEFORE he/she decides to purchase, what do they expect the food and delivery process to be like? In addition, the invoices can easily be emailed out from the system, and the purchase history is updated with the order in the CRM.

- **Production calculations:** Once recipes and specifications are entered into the software, the system will calculate how much of each item is needed to order and produce the catering order.
- **Labeling software:** The system can print labels for each order. Ensures a professional look and ease of setup and distribution of the food.
- **Operational checklists:** Typically an array of forms provided including production guides, packing lists, and driver setup checklist.

Since there is a monthly investment involved, operators need to weigh the cost and benefits of the monthly fee. Saving time no longer manually inputting data or doing calculations, order accuracy improvements, and professional labeling are all benefits of the software to be weighed against its cost. Do not overlook the importance of "opportunity cost" (aka TIME).

Too many managers and owners make the mistake of saving a few dollars by not having catering software because of the belief it can be done manually. While true, if a manager or owner spends three hours per week doing manual processes easily automated (and more accurately) by software, he/she could now have three hours per week to market catering. If the software costs $150 per month and saves the manager 12 hours per month, he/she could earn the restaurant 10x the investment if using that free time more wisely by being out—marketing catering vs. manually entering data.

CATERING BASICS

CHAPTER ACTION ITEMS

- Review financial terminology to ensure understanding by entire management/ownership team
- Evaluate group ordering opportunity
- Any additional ordering methods needed? Online, third-party, curbside
- Catering types offered—any changes needed? Pickup, drop-off, full-service
- Review additional potential third party vendors or services
- Determine "house account" and credit term/collection policies

CHAPTER 3
Financial Terminology

"The more you learn, the more you earn."
—Warren Buffet

THERE ARE MANY MISUNDERSTANDINGS around the finances of catering. Far too many operators have a negative bias toward catering since "It has a high cost of goods sold so costs increase." Yes, that statement is correct—costs, on a percentage basis, will likely increase. However, the bottom-line impact for the business is positive and needs to be understood. Catering should be embraced as one of the most effective ways to build top-line sales and bottom-line profit DOLLARS. Here are the common terms and definitions to ensure understanding and to provide the tools and knowledge to convince any skeptics in the company:

COGS $ (Cost of Goods Sold, Dollars)

COGS $ is the RAW COST the restaurant pays for the physical items, including food, beverage, paper, and packaging, used in the catering order. Some companies do not include paper in their calculation; in the examples throughout the book, however, it is included.

For example, a guest orders a Deluxe EZ Bundle: a tray of 10 sandwiches, a Cobb salad, 12 bags of chips, 12 cookies, and 12 canned drinks. To calculate the COGS $ of that order, add together the COST paid by the restaurant to make the 10 sandwiches, the Cobb salad, 12 chips, 12 cookies, the drinks, and then any packaging such as tray for the sandwiches, salad bowl, lid, tongs, dressing containers/spoons, and then plates, napkins, condiments, and any disposable bags to carry/serve the order. If these costs are not already calculated by item, now is the time.

FINANCIAL TERMINOLOGY

CATERING COGS EXAMPLE	
10 sandwiches	$18 ($1.80 ea x 10)
Cobb salad	$13
12 chips	$4.80 ($.40 ea)
12 cookies	$8.40 ($.70 ea)
12 canned drinks	$3.96 ($.33 ea)
Paper goods/packaging	$8.44 (total of all paper/disposable items)
Total COGS	**$58.60**

COGS % (Cost of Goods Sold, Percentage)

COGS % is the total dollar cost of the items used in the catering order divided by the selling price of the order to obtain the cost percent. In the example above, with a selling price for the Deluxe EZ Bundle of $155, the COGS % would be

$$\$58.60/\$155 = 37.8\%.$$

In most restaurants, catering COGS % is much higher than the COGS for regular menu items. This percentage in many cases causes the operator to NOT want to do catering as costs go up. While that is correct (i.e., costs do increase), the operator is tripping over dollars to pick up pennies. Why? Because of the dollar profit flow-thru generated from the order. More on flow-thru after understanding gross margin first.

Gross Margin

This is the sales price (in dollars) minus the COGS (in dollars). It is how many dollars made from selling the item or order. It is slightly different from bottom-line profit dollars. In this example, the gross margin is

$$(\text{selling price} - \text{COGS}) = \text{gross margin}$$
$$\$155 - \$58.60 = \$96.40$$

The restaurant made $96.40 in gross margin from this order. Yes, one

 *Catering Domination*

could argue there is labor involved, along with other costs such as royalties or credit card fees (further explanation under "flow-thru"). Had the order NOT been taken, the restaurant received $0 in sales, used $0 in products, and made $0 in profits. Since the order was accepted, the restaurant made $96.40 in gross margin (versus $0 in gross margin if the order was not accepted). Now let's look at *the* magic number: flow-thru.

Flow-Thru $ and %

Flow-thru is the incremental profit generated from the order versus if there was no sale or order). A good rule of thumb to follow is that, for every incremental sales dollar, the restaurant should make 50%–60% incremental profit. As an operator, every month sales are up, flow-thru should be calculated to ensure the team is "flowing thru" enough of the incremental sales to the bottom line.

To calculate flow-thru, take the incremental profit (from that order) and divide it by the sales (from that order). It is slightly different from gross margin, as it requires adding in any INCREMENTAL cost of that order, inclusive of third-party order/delivery fees, royalties (if the restaurant is a franchisee), credit card fees (if order was paid by credit card), and any additional labor incrementally needed to produce that order (in many cases there is not any extra labor needed). If there is a large order and extra labor is scheduled to produce the order, then, yes, those labor hours would be added into the costs.

Using the previous example, the following additional costs need to be added to the COGS to determine the incremental profit. DO NOT add in costs such as rent, electricity, and so on, as those costs are paid regardless of whether we get this order or not. In our case:

COGS $	$58.60 (cost of producing the order: food, beverage, paper/packaging)
Royalties	$7.75 (5% [or royalty amount] as example is franchised; $0 if corporate store)

FINANCIAL TERMINOLOGY

Credit card fees	$3.10 (2% is the cost to this business to accept credit cards)
Labor	$0.00 (no extra labor was needed to prepare this order)
Total Cost of Order	$69.45

Order Placed Directly with Restaurant

Flow-thru $ (profit from the order): $155 − $69.45 = $85.55

Flow-thru %: $85.55/$155 = 55.2%

Order Placed Directly with 3rd Party website

If ordered on an external site with a 25% fee, there is an $31 additional "cost"

Flow-thru $ (profit from order): $155 − $69.45 − 31 = $54.55

Flow-thru %: $54.55/$155 = 35%

In this example, 55% of this order flowed thru to the bottom line if placed direct with the restaurant or 35% if placed with an external website. Many restaurants do not like using a third-party catering site for orders, as the fees often range from 15%–30%. In the example above, if the fee is 25%, there is an additional cost of $31 for the third-party fee, so the profit after paying the fee is $54.55. The flow-thru in this case then becomes $54.55/$155 = 35%. While below the norm, even after paying the fee, the order generated over $54 in profit. Compared with $0 profit if the order is declined, it's a simple decision: take the order.

Yes, the COGS percentage will likely increase because of the catering order, but $85.55 (or $55 if ordered on a third party site) in BOTTOM-LINE PROFIT was generated from this order. Take the order. Promote catering. Catering is a welcomed addition due to the bottom-line profit impact it has on the operation. In our opinion, even if the order was a break-even (i.e., $0 profit), the order generated brand awareness and product trial, which should lead to sales down the road. Therefore, take the order as it is "free" marketing!

 Catering Domination

Catering Domination leads to profit domination and solid financial returns. Now that the solid foundation has been established, it's time to add the catering pillars.

> **CHAPTER ACTION ITEMS**
>
> ➢ *Review financial terminology to ensure understanding by entire management/ownership team*
>
> ➢ *Calculate COGS, Gross Margin, and Flow-Thru of catering items/orders to determine financial impact on sales and profits of catering*
>
> ➢ *Determine labor needed (if any) to flawlessly handle additional catering orders*

PART 2

The Catering Pillars

 *Catering Domination*

Erle Dardick and his team at Monkey Media Software and The Catering Institute did extensive work to layout the five pillars of catering. Erle granted permission to use these pillars in this book. After all, if a great foundation already exists, why reinvent one? The authors used these pillars as the basis for catering success—and enhanced them slightly after years of trial and error.

The pillars were updated due to ever-changing markets, vendors, technology, and finding new ways to dominate the catering space and vary slightly from the original five.

- Team Member Buy-In
- Marketing
- Sales
- Operations
- Delivery & Pickup
- Follow-Up

The next six chapters will explore each pillar in detail to ensure full understanding of why the pillar is critical and the benefits it can have on the catering business if executed properly. Let's dive in, catch some fish, and dominate the catering market.

PILLAR 1
Team Member Buy-In

"People will not actively commit to a decision if they have not had the opportunity to provide input, ask questions and understand the rationale behind it."
—Patrick Lencioni

WHEN WE FIRST FOCUSED ON CATERING after reading Erle's book on catering, leadership was all-in. The team (who was doing most of the work), however, viewed catering as a big headache. Seems life was a bit comfortable and though the ownership and leader of the restaurant understood the importance of catering (and additional hours for the team members), the team viewed the new business as a pain.

To help obtain team buy-in, two key items were launched:

1) About 30 days after catering sales ramped up, we sat down with the team to ask the group how we could make catering easier on them. They provided many insightful suggestions regarding prep and pre-work by the team at night, revamping par levels to eliminate some of the stress of trying to get the store open after all the catering was completed and some modifications to the offerings. Nearly every suggestion the team had made incredible sense ... and would allow us to book even more catering. To that end ...

2) We provided an incentive to everyone on the team to actively pursue catering sales for the restaurant. Anyone who secured a catering order would receive 10% of the order, even if it was a recurring order such as a school football team or band. We created a short "Every Guest Is an Opportunity" video to teach the team how to look beyond the "transaction" with the existing guests and start an "interaction" to uncover any catering needs they may have.

 Catering Domination

The results? While not every team member actively tried to secure catering orders, in fact, just a select few drove most of the growth. Here are a few examples of catering orders secured by the team in just a few short weeks:
- Middle-school basketball team's season-long orders totaled $4,800. The coach was in the restaurant w/logoed shirt on, and a supervisor talked to the coach about team meals ($480 check to the supervisor)
- High school debate coach ordered meals for a debate tournament totaling $2,950, as the team member saw the school district badge he was wearing ($295 check to her)
- Large distribution center placed a $5,100 order to feed the warehouse team, after a team member saw his name and company logo on his shirt and struck up a conversation ($510 check to her)

It takes a rare talent to sell though a simple training video to build confidence, along with an incentive to help the restaurant secure huge catering orders and nice incentive checks for those team members who helped. It also aligned with one of our values, "MBA—Mutually Beneficial for All". Guest wins (tries our food), restaurant wins (increased sales), and team member wins (additional pay).

If one is this far into the book, leadership buy-in to the idea of catering and wanting to generate more sales has been achieved. However, other managers and team members may view catering as a program that increases costs (false), requires additional capital or overhead (not necessary in most cases), or a nuisance interrupting operations (it can be if not designed, implemented, or trained properly—or lacks the proper systems). More on operational systems in a couple of chapters.

Meet with the decision-makers, ask for their input, provide the information on the following pages, and, for certain, meet with team members to solicit their thoughts and concerns. Operations needs frontline buy-in as well. As seen at the beginning of the chapter, leverage the front-line. Enlist the group to help sell catering as well as seek input on how to improve the catering production process. Did it cost me a little money? No. It cost me a lot of money. However, the restaurant made even more money on sales and profits from the efforts of the team. Everyday I hope an employee brings us

PILLAR 1: *Team Member Buy-In*

catering orders as I LOVE writing those incentive checks! In an effort to speed to a domination level, one needs to get buy-in up and down the ladder. To do so, the following keys need to be communicated clearly to ensure everyone understands why enhanced focus on catering is needed and their buy-in will be assured.

Financial Impact
Sales
As mentioned earlier, catering orders are typically larger in size and therefore generate top-line sales. It may seem far easier to obtain one $150 catering order than to obtain 20 new guests at $7.50 to order from the restaurant. Depth over width.

Another ancillary benefit of catering and group orders is that the meals are consumed outside the restaurant, generating sales outside the four walls. Not only does a catering order help keep more tables open for dine-in guests, the cleanup necessary for in-store dining is not needed, either. Catering raises sales and improves the guest experience.

Flow-Thru & Profitability
Even though COGS on catering orders is usually higher than items on the regular menu (percentage wise), the flow-thru profitability of catering orders drives the bottom-line profit dollars. Customize the examples provided earlier with data from the restaurant to illustrate to nonbelievers why catering is an important sales and profit generator. Catering raises profit dollars.

Labor
Most catering orders do not have an impact on labor costs. An average $150–$200 catering order can normally be produced without adding labor hours. Adding the $150–$200 to sales for the day without any labor actually lowers labor cost. Though larger orders may require additional labor, usually the labor percentage on catering orders (not including full-service off-site

catering) runs in the 10%–12% range. Catering lowers labor cost.

When selling catering's importance up the chain of command, talk dollars and cents. Leadership must understand those terms. Driving top-line lines and raising bottom-line profits gets the attention and resources one needs. Build the incentive cost into the labor model and ensure the team is being rewarded so they are excited about the catering increase.

Marketing Impact

Another critical benefit of catering is the marketing impact it has by building brand awareness and trial. Best news of all? Guests pay to be marketed to.

Brand Awareness

Many guests who attend catered meetings or functions may not even be aware of the restaurant—or they may be aware but have not yet tried the food. Either way, catering creates brand awareness by introducing the brand to those attending the event. Keep in mind that the restaurant is getting paid for its ability to create brand awareness when catering. What other marketing pays to market the brand?

School catering (and catering in general) is a huge brand-awareness builder, especially for newer restaurants. When a parent (local office or retailer) sees the order form or online link to order team or group meals for a child, he/she not only now knows the brand but sees the brand engaged in the local community and supporting their kids. Next time the family is going out to eat, the brand is on the tip of their tongue.

Next, any catering marketing helps build brand awareness. While many operators complain about the fees paid for third-party delivery and catering sites, remember, when a potential catering guest logs into the third-party app or website, the restaurant's logo appears. The guest may scroll through and view the menu and learn about the brand. While that buyer may or may not choose the restaurant to cater to their needs today, the brand is now in mental shelf space of the guest for future catering orders. The cost to the restaurant for that brand awareness? Zero.

PILLAR 1: *Team Member Buy-In*

Trial

The next marketing impact catering can have on the business is trial. First, the guest is trying the food as they are at the catered meeting or event. Bingo! They have the restaurant's food in their mouths—and the restaurant got paid for that trial. Second, deliver coupons for all attendees with a call-to-action for them to order online or visit the restaurant. Now the guest will have tried the restaurant two times. Alternatively, if coupons are not the way the brand wants to go, promote the loyalty app, online ordering, or other ways the catering attendees can engage in the brand and experience it.

As illustrated later in the book, obtaining a catering trial is the first step toward securing any catering order for the brand. Once the catering client tries the food, the restaurant will experience the impact of that catering, thereby building brand awareness and trial. Therefore, it is recommended to do a targeted feet-on-the-street campaign focused on catering trial. Pick a "business of the day" winner. Surprise that company (hint: pick companies that are likely to be catering buyers.). Drop off a catering tray and a couple boxed meals along with catering marketing materials (and some coupons) to introduce potential catering buyers to the brand. Ideal targets are doctor's offices, big-box retailers, apartment complexes, schools, chamber meetings (offer to cater for free), and car dealers just to name a few. Search "largest employers" around the restaurant and start contacting them.

Menu

In many restaurants, the catering menu varies from the in-store menu. While many items may be offered on the catering and regular menu, often the catering menu is different. The brand can be impacted greatly by not creating an effective catering menu reflective of the brand's positioning and expertise. Many reading this book will not have authority to change or create the catering menu, but providing feedback to the decision makers is recommended.

There is a huge marketing risk to the brand if the catering menu is not created properly. Items offered on the catering menu should be the brand's

 *Catering Domination*

signature and mainstay items (assuming they travel well) not simply an array of catering items one believes catering buyers would want. As an example, Chick-fil-A offers potato chips in its boxed meals instead of French fries. The brand realizes fries do not travel well and, therefore, does not include them as part of their catering offering—even though many people love its waffle fries.

Being in the sandwich business the "signature tray" is a key item to be promoted versus a "traditional tray." The traditional tray has ham, turkey, and other choices every other sandwich tray has on it. Promoting the signature with an Italian grinder, Buffalo chicken, and more unique sandwiches drives the likelihood of helping the brand stand out and drives further trial and in-store visits. Promote unique items—do not provide what others provide. Provide and recommend signature items. Catering domination.

Since many people are experiencing the brand for the first time through a catered meal, it's imperative from a brand and marketing standpoint that the menu is spot-on, high-quality, and executed to exacting brand standards. After all, if the guest tries the food at a catered event and doesn't like it, what are the chances he/she will visit the restaurant?

Operational Impact

One of the greatest concerns, and it should be, is the impact catering production has on normal restaurant operations. Catering is a different business. It is producing larger amounts of food to be consumed off-site while not interrupting in-store service. There are a few operational benefits and a number of pitfalls to avoid.

As stated earlier, leverage the knowledge of the team members who are producing the catering orders. There is a good chance they know improvements that can be made ... if only someone will ask! Some of these we painfully uncovered so pay attention here and avoid the pain we felt!

PILLAR 1: *Team Member Buy-In*

Benefits to Operations
Building Off-Hour Sales/Providing Additional Labor Hours

Catering expands the shoulders of the business, as many catering orders are delivered just prior to, or after, the lunch rush (and dinnertime as well). A successful catering program can also generate the sales increases necessary to provide more labor hours for team members. Hours are needed to do additional prep for catering and building boxed meals for the next day or staging of supplies for the following days' orders.

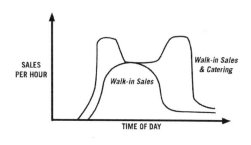

Production Times

Production times for lunchtime catering orders can be often done prior to the rush, while school team (midafternoon deliveries) and dinner catering orders can be produced after the lunch rush. While the restaurant may receive last-minute catering orders in the middle of a rush, most often the orders can be worked in around the normal daily prep and production schedule and smooth out operations.

Career Path

Catering is a great opportunity to provide leadership development and a career path. Building catering sales to a level requiring a salesperson (or more) or a catering manager to oversee production and deliveries provides opportunities for people to grow into new roles, learn new skills, and earn more money. Centralized services (covered in Pillar 3) is a recommended strategy and allows for career pathing as described.

Catering Challenges

Catering's operational challenges are numerous and must be thought through and addressed in advance to ensure buy-in from everyone. Engage

 *Catering Domination*

the team members to help solve these challenges to prevent them from derailing the program:

- Space constraints requiring creative solutions to store additional catering supplies.
- Production lines often were not designed to produce large catering orders while also making food for the dine-in guests. How can both catering and dine-in production happen flawlessly?
- Catering requires additional supplies such as packaging, hot boxes, insulated bags, marketing materials, cold transport bags, and heightened food safety (even outside the four walls).
- Catering requires more logistics than a typical dine-in or to-go order; longer production times; additional prep completed the day prior to the order; storage space for paper goods and packaging; adequate cold and hot storage for larger orders; longer sell cycle; following-up after the order.
- Delivery (if done in-house) requires additional scheduling and hiring/insurance requirements.

If the catering program does not currently exist, an effective one must be created. An outside expert can be enlisted if needed. Talk with the food distributor, as it typically possesses the resources to help. What catering items can be created with existing products? What additional packaging requirements are necessary? What menu items should NOT be part of catering as the product doesn't travel or hold up well? Remember, catering is a different business. Study the competition, talk to catering buyers, find out what they buy and why.

The last and most important point is staff buy-in. The best way to get team commitment is to ask what they think about catering, how to sell more, how to ensure smooth production and implementation, and, finally, to reinforce the business case for why we need catering. Allowing staff input at this critical juncture ensures they have ownership in the program and will help support its success.

That is just the first pillar—and you already have a ton of information to digest. Stop. Breathe. You. Can. Dominate. Evaluate the current catering

PILLAR 1: *Team Member Buy-In*

program and modify as needed. Ensure buy-in and commitment up and down the chain of command. If buy-in is not in place yet, get it created before moving to the next chapter. Once the program is in place, everyone is ready to proceed, then it's time to promote it.

CHAPTER ACTION ITEMS

➢ *Review financial impact, menu, and operational needs with leadership after you:*

- *Meet with the team members to uncover opportunities and challenges catering has on operations*

- *Create a short sales-training video covering how to identify potential catering guests in the restaurant and how to find school contacts or visit local retailers (covered later in the book) to give the team confidence to sell ... and earn an additional incentive.*

- *Design incentive program for securing catering orders (keep it simple: 10% works; perhaps bump it to 20% during slower periods to help smooth the decline in sales)*

PILLAR 2
Marketing

"People buy from people they like."
—Tom Walker

AS MENTIONED EARLIER, securing catering orders is like fishing. Having targeted clients ensures it is fishing in a barrel versus in an ocean. Sales and marketing, however, are not the same thing. Marketing tactics are like chumming the waters; that is, leading the prospects to the product. In the case of fishing, it is attracting the right fish to the boat to make it easier to catch them.

Sales tactics are equivalent to putting numerous fishing poles with hooks and the right bait in the chummed waters and reel in the fish. In catering terminology, "sales tactics" are things such as lunch-n-learn catering presentations, bringing free meals to the coaching staff at a school, or providing samples at an event of targeted buyers.

Marketing informs and attracts leads and prospects to the company's product. Marketing encompasses the strategies used to reach new leads and generate interest in the business. Outbound marketing and brand awareness are necessary but often expensive and not as targeted, especially when trying to identify and contact catering buyer. Sales is working directly with targeted prospects to convert those prospects into paying guests. Sales is the process of actually convincing someone to buy from the business. Typically, sales is a result of marketing efforts.

Initially, focus on lower-hanging fruit (the kind hanging so low that it is kicked as one walks) versus more expensive list purchases and brand building. Most restaurants cannot afford outbound marketing, as it is like throwing a net over the side of the boat and hoping to catch the desired fish wanted.

PILLAR 2: *Marketing*

The list of sales and marketing tactics recommended is presented below. Keep in mind that not every tactic is right for every restaurant—nor can all these items be done all at the same time. Rather, map out a strategy of which tactics will be utilized. Vary the ones used over time to identify which tactics are the most effective for the restaurant. They include the following.

MARKETING TACTICS	
Operational Marketing	**External Marketing**
Catering Website	Buying Lists
Phone	Digital Ads
Third-Party Catering Websites	Social Media
Local Events	Postcards & Direct Mail
Feet-on-the-Street	Click Funnels
	Third-Party Street Teams
	Google Alerts
Relationship Tactics	***Sales Tactics*** *(see next chapter, Pillar 3)*
Networking, Chamber of Commerce & Local Associations	Existing Guests
New Event Venues/Hotels	Fishbowl
New Real Estate Developments	Building Lists
	Targeted Groups
	Targeted Sampling
	Lunch-N-Learns
	Swag & Perks for Buyers

Let's examine each in more detail, so a determination can be made which ones to use initially and which ones to use down the road. They have been divided into marketing, relationship, and sales tactics to illustrate which ones are more focused on brand-building and finding prospects (marketing) and which are more targeted toward converting a prospect into a catering buyer.

 *Catering Domination*

Marketing Tactics

These tactics are broken into three parts: first, operational approaches to marketing (e.g., things that can be done by operations, or with a little bit of support for ops). Second, more traditional marketing approaches, and, third, relationship marketing. In all cases, these tactics are trying to build awareness of the catering offerings and trying to generate interest in the catering. Think of these strategies as speed dating—meeting many people for a short time and trying to find those interested in pursuing things further. These tactics help identify which companies can be targeted once interest is expressed.

Operational Marketing Tactics

These tactics are items done by operations or support focused primarily on the restaurant team using its products and resources to help promote catering and the brand to groups and companies near the restaurant. They differ from sales tactics (covered in Pillar 3), as those are more targeted toward companies or people known to have a need to buy catering.

To have a chance even to compete in the catering game, the restaurant must have:

- Catering specific website
- Great phone skills
- Presence on third-party catering sites

Catering Website

The catering website must be easy to navigate for a buyer (and highlighted predominantly on the home page) and have the proper keywords on the site to be optimized for search engines to find and rank the site high when guests are searching for catering. Ad words are discussed later in this chapter, but those come at a significant expense.

Ensure the site is designed to promote popular and profitable catering offerings and package deals. Make it easy for the person to click "Order Now."

PILLAR 2: *Marketing*

Phone

Guests still continue to call and inquire about or order catering. In many restaurants, however, the phone is a nuisance and ignored or answered poorly. Think a catering client would want to order from a restaurant that cannot answer the phone properly or provide the courtesy of a professionally handled call? These guests are spending well over $150 (and often much more). At minimum, have a fun on-hold message directing the guest to order catering online while he/she waits for someone to return to the call. Remember, it is "hold" not "ignore"—get back to the call quickly.

If the restaurant is busy, get the guest's name and number and let him/her know that the catering manager will call back shortly. Let the guest know you are interested in serving their needs and want the catering expert to handle this important call. DO NOT make the guest call back; he/she will simply call the competitor.

Some restaurants forward the phones to an answering service during peak hours, while even others have a catering call center to take the orders away from the hustle and bustle of the busy restaurant.

Taking the phone to the next level, have a dedicated catering number. Free numbers can be can obtained from Google. Set it to forward to the owner, catering manager, or whomever is leading the catering. As Nordstrom's says, "How people define customer service—that is where the battle will continue to be won and lost."

Never rush taking an order. Catering orders often have many variables, and it is easy to make a mistake. There is also an opportunity to build that relationship, and it cannot be risked trying to take a phone order while dealing with in-store guests. Additionally, if, while taking the order, you rush to get the guest off the phone, opportunities to upsell profitable add-ons will be missed. Return the call ASAP after the rush. Apologize for missing the call but devote full attention now. It will be appreciated by the guest, as the entire focus is on their order.

Answer the phone! "MONEY" is calling.

 Catering Domination

Third-Party Catering Websites

As mentioned previously, many operators frown upon third-party catering sites due to the fees charged. However, not many things can be marketed for free. These sites are one of those options. Simply signing up and getting the restaurant logo and menu on sites such as these cost nothing. FREE marketing. Potential buyers are seeing the logo and menu. Even if no orders are ever received, free exposure has been received. The other reasons why these sites need to be part of the marketing efforts have been explained, and it is financially a win for the restaurant.

Local Events

While this approach takes time and minor expense, getting in front of guests and potential guests is a battle. A great opportunity is to have a brand presence at as many local events as possible. Have a branded tent and tables set up to sample food (if allowed) and pass out branded swag. Additionally, have catering information, menus, and bounce-back coupons to invite people into the restaurant. Great events to attend include parades, races, wine walks, "taste of ...," kids festivals, and so on.

Take it to the next level. Have a prize wheel the attendees can spin to win free prizes; have the person wanting to spin fill out a contact info form to build the database. If no prize wheel, have a QR code or tablet to do instant signups (like a virtual "fishbowl") to collect their information in return for a chance to win a catered lunch for 10 people. Now the person becomes a targeted prospect to sell the amazing catering.

Feet-on-the-Street

Feet on the street (aka "canvassing") is an effective marketing strategy to quickly generate targeted prospects for the catering sales pipeline. Budget five hours of labor per week for four weeks to hit all the areas around the restaurant. Use one hour per day to do feet-on-the-street marketing.

Break the area into quadrants and hit one area from 10–11 A.M. or 2–3 P.M. each day. Layout the trade around the restaurant and identify retail stores, offices, hospitals, office parks, and other companies to visit. Have

PILLAR 2: *Marketing*

the person doing the canvassing armed with the following:
- Business card of the catering manager (or designated catering contact)
- Bounce-back coupons: provide one for each employee
- Catering menus
- Small samples such as desserts or signature chips (or small portions of other unique items, ideally prepackaged)
- Swag for the company (reusable plastic cups are awesome leave-behinds to advertise the brand or a few $5 gift cards the company can use as a perk)

Visit the designated quadrant for the day, ask for the manager, and provide the coupons, catering menus, and swag. Find out who (if anyone) coordinates catering (*and* group ordering) and get this person's business card or contact information. Not all companies will utilize catering (or group ordering), but ensure those contacts who do cater have their information entered into the CRM or spreadsheet.

Take it to the next level. Provide a "FRACTION OF THE ACTION" by rewarding those doing feet on the street with a 10% incentive of any catering order placed by a company that was visited.

External Marketing
Buying Lists
Lists are available online to purchase contact information of the companies located around the restaurant. Simply search "companies" (or businesses in my area) for companies who provide lists (most are for purchase). Filters can be used to better fine-tune the database of contacts. For example, select companies with a minimum size of ten people, radius of three miles from the location, and so on. Lists are beneficial to be used for mailing lists as well as to identify key companies and business locations around the restaurant to inquire about catering needs.

This tactic is pure outbound marketing, as the interest level in catering is not known, and money and time will be spent on companies that may or may not be catering guests.

 *Catering Domination*

Digital Basics

Digital marketing is perhaps the most cost-effective tools in marketing. At the 2020 Illinois Restaurant Association Tech Tour, Google provided the following advice to restaurant operators—for restaurants to be successful and win in the digital age, they need to do the following with their website, mobile sites, and digital presence:

- Create Awareness
- Inspire Desire
- Grab Attention to Get Noticed

Awareness is how the consumer in this competitive landscape of distractions and ads becomes aware of the brand. The customer needs to know if the business is open, what are the hours, and any special closures. When does the restaurant deliver? Does the restaurant offer catering?

The number one search on "NEAR ME" from 2015–2019 is "restaurants". Is the restaurant's website and social sites named and correctly setup for Google? Some catering customers will secretly shop the restaurant before placing catering orders. They are going to call and order a lunch or two, stop by the restaurant, and see what the basic services and experience.

Many guests dining in the restaurant are on their phone. In 2019, "inside restaurants" searches have increased to 15%. Guests are looking for photos, nutritional information, specials, and Google Reviews. Deliver great service so the reviews are positive—and reply quickly to any that are less than five-star.

Prior to COVID-19, Google reported the following:

- 75% of all search is done on Google;
- 54% of restaurant searches are looking for hours of operations
- 42% of guests go right to the "directions" button after the initial search
- Restaurants were receiving 6x more queries for "pickup" than "delivery"
- "Order online" from Google My Business is getting 10x the number of uses than any other button
- Google is deploying an online order for pickup and catering

PILLAR 2: *Marketing*

In the ever-changing technology space, start with Google. How does Google connect guests?
- Google Maps—check the restaurant's listing to ensure information is correct.
- Google Assistant is its answer to those who use Alexa and Siri
- Google Android Auto Service is making waves via its ability to order via smart TVs

Next, ensure the restaurant's Google My Business page is claimed and being utilized. It is free.
- Ensure the page has current photos and is using a "Google Offer"
- Is the business verified?
- Site provides marketing information such as which zip codes people are from that are searching the business as well as data on photo views and rank versus local competition
- Site also provides when guests call from the Google button

Lesson here? Ensure the Google page is set up and data points are being leveraged.

Digital Ads

With advancements in digital and social networking, one can dial-in guest demographics. The key with digital catering ads is to create a compelling offer and target to the right audience. Next, select the right audience to target. If targeting admins in the 25–54 age bracket, research titles in their profiles (event planners, executive admin, administrative professionals). Where do they live and work? Target the ads based on these demographics. Do not spend more than $20 per target until the right groups are identified. Facebook Business Manager is a free tool and will easily help dial in the digital ad strategy to determine which ads and targeted groups are most effective.

Social Media

Most restaurateurs are not comfortable with social media. According to the 2019 Restaurant Success Industry Report by Toast, 12% of restaurateurs do not bother with marketing at all. Restaurateurs typically have a love/hate relationship with Facebook. The platform's algorithm has undergone many changes that have affected how consumers see posts from pages. Many restaurants treat their Facebook page as their website. Instagram is showing a growth trajectory in popularity with restaurateurs and sites, such as TikTok (and undoubtedly others since the book was printed), take share away from proven social sites.

Social Content

Rule #1: Content must be authentic. Yes, sprinkle in the fancy food photography, but people want to see real food and real people's stories and motivations. Stick with major social platforms such as Facebook, Instagram, LinkedIn, and Google My Business. Video postings are a must. High usage times for social media in the restaurant space are just prior to lunch hour.

What makes great social posts?

- Stories and sharing team members in action
- Telling the brand story
- Providing value deals
- Showcasing, participating and/or sharing community events
- Showcasing customer success
- Pictures of catering delivery, setup, and execution

What causes social media misery?

- Avoid politics and religion (and sports)
- Avoid photos that would alarm a health inspector
- Avoid making light of negative current events
- Avoid posting photos of catering clients' offices or logos; do not let the competition know where the restaurant is "fishing"

Social posts are a billboard for LIFE. Build the brand narrative and celebrate the team and guest. Engage the guests to become part of the brand.

PILLAR 2: *Marketing*

Postcards & Direct Mail

Postcards and direct mail work for coupons to promote online ordering or in-store dining but are less effective for catering orders—until NOW. Using the lists bought or built greatly enhances the chance of coupon redemption from the mailers. Additionally, using a service, such as Every Door Direct Mailers (EDDM), help push the redemption rates higher.

A focused series of postcards to the catering audience will have a higher redemption rate. Have a cadence on mailing. Send postcards every two weeks for a total of eight weeks. After the second or third mailer, follow up with a call or surprise-and-delight drop-off. Create a specific postcard with a strong call to action. Motivate the recipient with an offer too good to refuse with a limited time and limited number. The offer should feed at least 10 people and put the value of that feeding on the card.

The differences between a good and great postcard are as follows:
- Great food and product photos
- Great offer with NO catch with a value, for limited time or number
- Direct catering phone number (not the store number)
- Neat, handwritten address in colored ink versus a label and a real stamp
- Drop in the mail on FRIDAY

Why so specific? Great photos catch attention. Personal touches, such as handwritten and a stamp, are noticed.

Why Friday? The postcard will be received Monday or Tuesday, when the catering decisions are being made. If postcards are mailed Monday or Tuesday, they arrive Thursday and Friday, and the week's catering opportunities are gone and will be forgotten over the weekend.

Postcards and mailers can get expensive. Do not mail all at one time or to a large area, as the restaurant will have to be able to handle the pitch for those who respond. Keep the mailers targeted and at a steady cadence. With an effective list or geographical area, redemption rates of 6% to 10% can happen (compared with the industry norm of 2%).

Click Funnels

Click funnels, also known as "sales funnels," are web pages created for the purpose of landing leads, selling products, collecting email registrations, or promoting services. These pages are called "lead generation pages" and use specific formulas to get visitors to complete an action such as giving us their email and information on catering needs.

Think of this strategy as a digital postcard. It is a single page that causes the user to give his/her information in exchange for something. Make the funnel simple and able to be created on virtually any web hosting platform. For a good example, check out www.winfreecatering.com. Buy a similar type of domain name (e.g., www.win[brandname]freecatering.com) to direct guests and start the funnel process.

Click funnels work by creating multiple "call to actions" a visitor has to act upon such as providing catering information, signing up for a loyalty program, or placing an order. Once a visitor lands on the catering funnel, promote the brand and catering with the call to action. By placing it above the fold, the user is inclined to complete the action or read more. Food photography and action shots help persuade the visitor to complete an action. Click funnels work because they usually offer a free product combined with a paid service or product.

Promote the website at local events, on the fishbowl in store, in digital ads, email blasts, and social media posts to get a high number of participants going to the website and providing the information.

Stay on top of the data entered, add it to the CRM or spreadsheet, and start prospecting, as these guests have expressed an interest in catering.

Third-Party Street Teams

Vendors such as Field Day (www.fieldday.app) and others can help do some of the legwork of feet-on-the-street efforts for the restaurant. Whether doing phone outreach or targeted visits to local businesses, third-party street teams can help collect interested prospects for the restaurants. There is a cost associated with these services but the investment may be worth it by generating catering orders and future prospects.

PILLAR 2: *Marketing*

Google Alerts
Google Alerts can be setup to notify you when specific phrases pop up on the web such as what your competitors are doing. Setup an alert for the top catering competitors' brands to keep an eye on what they are doing in the catering space.

Relationship Tactics
The following tactics are "marketing"—they are used to reach new leads and generate interest in the business. Typically, these will include the local chamber of commerce (joining multiple ones might be necessary depending on where the guests come from), local government or associations, and the convention and visitors' bureau. To reach these new leads and generate interest from these group about catering, work the room. Build relationships, network, get to know decision-makers around the area. Give back! Volunteer to help local causes—not only because the favors will be returned, but because it is the right thing to do.

Networking, Chamber of Commerce & Local Associations
Join the chamber of commerce, restaurant association, convention and visitor bureau, Kiwanis, United Way, and so on. Similar to joining a health club, however, joining does not change results. Too many times a person joins but neither gets involved nor networks. People join these organizations because they believe in their cause. The collective power is stronger than the individual. When getting involved in these organizations, a person not only serves the spirit of group but also the community and each other. Members are Main Street Americans trying to improve the communities and themselves. The key to being involved in a membership-based organization is contributing to the betterment of the group—not just paying lip-service and signing the check.

All these groups' members need to eat. They have personal parties and businesses and are involved in other community groups that need catering. The opportunity is huge, but it takes commitment, time, and patience. Get involved, show up at the meetings, donate catering to the networking

events, or host a meeting at the restaurant. Showcase the business. Get involved! Network and build relationships. People buy from those they trust. Be the person others trust.

Typically, the group's membership fee includes the contact list, social media opportunities to promote members' businesses, and many other low-cost marketing opportunities such as newsletters and e-blasts. The groups want their members to be engaged and successful. Each member needs as many additional advocates as possible. Most importantly, build relationships while helping others—and those relationships could transfer the catering business.

When working with members of these groups, ensure others can put a name to a face. Having a business relationship with the restaurant or catering manager is a huge advantage versus the competition. Having the inside track is similar to being able to fish the best spots before the competition even hears about it.

Effective marketing leads to the next pillar: sales. Remember, marketing *informs* and *attracts* leads and prospects to the company's product. Sales is working directly with *targeted prospects* to convert those prospects into paying guests. Time to convert some sales.

New Event Venues & Hotels

New event venues and hotels should be contacted prior to their opening. Find out what type of events they host and typical group sizes. Larger venues (and hotels) either have their own caterer or allow "preferred vendors" to service the venue—find out how to get on that list! Smaller, limited-service hotels often do not have their own in-house caterer or restaurant so be the first vendor on their list to recommend to the meetings they host.

New Real Estate Developments

See a sign for a new office park, hospital, medical center, or shopping center "under construction" or "coming soon"? Visit the construction foreman to discuss feeding those building the center. Research online or contact the developer to get a tenant list so you are ready to contact them once they open for business. New fishing hole!

PILLAR 2: *Marketing*

CHAPTER ACTION ITEMS

- Ensure website is updated and easy to use for guests
- Phone answer and selling training provided to all employees. Validate skills and knowledge
- Prioritize marketing strategies and tactics to be used
- Outside assistance needed (for digital ads, street team versus team members doing, etc.)
- Determine budget and ROI targets for each tactic and overall sales goal

PILLAR 3: Sales

"Once you replace negative thoughts with positive ones, you'll start having positive results."
—Willie Nelson

ONCE THE GUEST HAS TAKEN THE BAIT (aka, the marketing message), it is time to reel him/her in. Marketing has laid the foundation and helped provide a pipeline of targeted prospects. It is nearly time to close the deal. However, a more detailed understanding of sales is needed to ensure catering domination.

First, effective sales tactics must be practiced. Some might argue these tactics are really "marketing", but "sales" was split out from marketing, as the tactics in this chapter are focused on people or groups who are already targeted prospects. These include:

- In-store guests
- In-store messaging
- Building lists
- Targeted groups
- Targeted sampling
- Swag and perks for buyers

Next, there must be an effective sales process to include:

- The pitch
- Order taking—dedicated catering phone number and email address
- Customer Relationship Manager (CRM)

Let's start with the sales tactics to see what additional barrels, stocked to the brim with easy-to-catch fish, should be utilized.

PILLAR 3: *Sales*

Sales Tactics
In-Store Guests
Existing guests are a great place to fish. The guests already love the food—now get them to love the catering. Teach the team to talk to guests and identify clues to make the conversation natural and personal. If wearing a lanyard or logoed shirt with a business or school name, ask if they have any catering needs (or can provide the contact person's name and phone or email).

Teach the mindset of "Every Guest Is an Opportunity." Learn where the guests work or if they have any catering needs for kids, teams, groups, churches, fundraisers. One will likely uncover parents involved in kids' groups, those who are pharma reps, coaches, or work in other areas that have catering needs. Talk about a competitive advantage—these guests are in the restaurant (not the competitor's) right now. Use the clues.

In-Store Messaging
Point-of-Purchase Material (P.O.P.)
Create (with brand's approval if needed) catchy, disruptive pieces to promote catering. Too often restaurants have tired, dirty table tents, danglers from the ceiling, or cluttered messaging at the cashier area (or no catering messaging at all). Be disruptive; think differently. Where do the guests stare the most?

Many quick-serve or fast casual restaurants have vast space on walls behind the cashier or pickup area—prime real estate for disruptive catering messages. Set up a small table in the restaurant with a sample catering setup and brochures or place the advertising on the mirror or the inside of the door of the restrooms so guests do not miss the messaging when exiting the restroom. Be different to dominate.

Bounce-Back Coupons
Provide a catering bounce-back in third-party deliveries and online orders. Also, include bounce-back coupons for in-store dining or online ordering in

 *Catering Domination*

all catering orders. Win both ways. Generating sales from a catering order is awesome—but it can be even more powerful if additional guests start ordering online or visiting the restaurant as a result of the coupon provided when they tried the catering. Mark the coupon with the company or group name of the catering so results can be tracked. Return on investment.

Fishbowl
A strategy as old as time but proven effective still today. Place the fishbowl at an obvious spot for the guest to see. Provide a "free sampling for 10" for the winning name. Hint: EVERYONE will be a winner, albeit some with smaller prizes. Since many people no longer carry business cards, have a QR code or a "contact info" slip of paper guests can use to "enter." Pick a winner weekly or monthly depending on the quantity of entries. Ensure all contacts are entered into the Customer Relationship Manger (CRM) or spreadsheet.

Building Lists
While buying lists is less time-consuming and easy (but expensive), building targeted lists is likely more cost effective and will generate a much greater return on the investment. Lists can be built from the feet-on-the-street or fishbowl efforts previously mentioned. As a good fishermen researches where the best fishing holes are so, too, should an effective manager. The next part of the chapter covers targeted groups and events. Building lists to enter in the CRM or spreadsheet is a crucial step to stay ahead of the catering competition.

First, identify the key targets around the restaurant. Schools and events typically have easily searchable websites with contact names, numbers, and emails. Searching local retailers or companies is often more difficult to obtain key contacts and their emails or phone numbers. If school and team catering (they need boxed lunches) are a target, search the school district and local school, then obtain the following contacts to add to the CRM or spreadsheet:
- Principal
- Principal's secretary or office administrator

PILLAR 3: *Sales*

- Coaches (e.g., football, volleyball, basketball, track, baseball, softball, swimming, and any other sport, who might need team meals)
- Fine arts/group directors (e.g., band, theater, choir, orchestra, drumline, debate, drill team, and cheerleading)
- PTA (e.g., to book fundraisers or help school raise funds, even through catering)

Churches are another list easily built by searching online for positions, such as youth director (offer to donate vacation bible school coupons during the summer), adult group contacts, and so on, as these groups often need catering. Add these contacts to the CRM or spreadsheet. Who should be targeted to build these lists?

Targeted Groups

As mentioned in the previous section, building lists of targeted groups is done through online searching for schools, churches, and other groups. Feet-on-the-street can also help provide a list of targeted groups, primarily retail stores, local medical, car dealers, dental and veterinary, banks, CPAs, and so on.

Enter these contacts into the CRM or spreadsheet and ensure there is a column for business type (retail, school, car dealer, etc.), so this information can easily be sorted and used for targeted (and timely) messaging. For example, contact:

- Retail locations in October for Black Friday and holiday catering
- School coaches and directors targeted in advance of their season or needs
- School administrators prior to in-service or testing days, as well as prior to Teacher Appreciation Week (offer an in-store deal that week for teachers, donate gift cards for prizes)

Whom should be targeted around the restaurant? Here are a few groups to consider for catering domination.

Schools/Groups

Contact the band, booster clubs, drama, sports teams, teachers, tournaments

Catering Domination

at schools (debate, band, sporting events, choir, theater, swim, track), meet the teacher/open house, fundraiser nights (promote catering during the entire week of a fundraiser event to generate larger sales for the fundraiser and promote catering), and the administration for meetings and other catering opportunities.

Car Dealers
Drop off boxed lunch samples midweek to the catering buyer (usually receptionist or sales manager) along with bounce-back coupons. While there, find out their budget. Dealers usually have a $5–$7 per person budget but are buying meals every Saturday in quantities of 50 to 100 or more. Want another $500–$700 in the register prior to the lunch rush on a Saturday? Stay in contact with the decision-maker to ensure the restaurant is part of the dealer's catering rotation.

Retail/Big Box Stores
Visit the location and ask for the manager or HR manager. Provide a stack of coupons for the employees to use in-store or online. Catering needs for retailers during the holiday season: Black Friday through New Year's Day (though catering is often ordered for inventory night), staff meetings, training sessions, and product launches at smaller retailers such as phone and gaming stores.

Pharma Reps
This category is time and organizational-sensitive. Pharma reps typically call a doctor's office, ask what type of catering the group wants, and orders it. The rep makes a short presentation, while the staff is enjoying the catering. The last thing the reps need is to deal with catering issues. To be successful in this segment, here are the main keys:
- **On time is LATE.** There is too much competition, and, once that trust is broken, the rep will not be heard from again. Be early or be forgotten. Arrive early to set up as well as meet and build a relationship with the office staff. They are the gate keepers to further

PILLAR 3: *Sales*

pharma rep referral business (or additional direct orders).
- **Pharma reps demand trust.** They appreciate a caterer who is on time and sets up the catering so the rep can focus on making the presentation.
- **Creative setup.** Most caters simply "drop and dash". Medical offices can be a bit more challenging to set up. Medical breakrooms were not designed for catering. Offices are typically a maze. Ensure the team is prepared and early to deal with the additional setup time
- **Payment.** Pharma reps will all use credit cards, as they must have an audit trail based on the Sunshine Act. This act requires drug and device manufacturers to disclose to the Secretary of Health and Human Services (HHS), on a quarterly basis, anything of value given to physicians, such as payments, gifts, honoraria, or travel. Stiff penalties can be assessed to the rep and company for noncompliance.
- **Payment recording.** Detailed payment recording ensures if the pharma rep ever needs a receipt, the restaurant has it. Having a CRM eases this process as the order can be stored along with the credit card number and invoice copy. If using a spreadsheet, ensure the order is entered, along with the date and total, so if a receipt ever needs to be resent, it can easily be found in the POS system and reprinted.

Pharma reps deal with countless offices. These reps are huge advocates (and sales-generators) for the restaurants they trust.

Targeted Sampling

Once targeted prospects have been identified from the fishbowl or feet-on-the-street, it is time to select winners (aka the "Business of the Day [or Week]"). Randomly (as in ones with most catering potential) select a local business as the winner and provide a WOW Box, which is a smaller sample of catering offerings (sandwich tray or entree, salad or side, boxed meals if offered, or sweets and desserts).

Show up to the location around 11 A.M. and let the business know it won. Provide the restaurant business card or contact info in the box and find the person who orders catering for the business. It's a small cost and expense, but sales is all about enticing a targeted prospect to buy from the restaurant.

Catering Domination

For those who entered the fishbowl but were not selected, send them a consolation prize such as a gift card or free meal in the restaurant.

Lunch-N-Learns
Once orders are received from a school or large office, ask that client if he/she will contact all the other catering buyers there and let the restaurant cater in a free lunch for the group in return for a short presentation on the catering offerings (aka Lunch-N-Learn). These events are a great way to have the decision-makers try the product risk-free and make a personal connection with the catering contact or manager; it also provides an opportunity for numerous buyers to be added to the prospect list. It's like fishing in a well-stocked barrel.

Swag & Perks for Buyers
Many restaurants offer discounts on catering orders. While they may entice a consumer to purchase a catering tray or a few boxed lunches, administrators ordering for a company or pharma reps buying for doctors' offices are not concerned with discounts (as long as the budget is maintained). What excites these buyers are perks such as gift cards for other businesses (e.g., Amazon gift card). Entice catering buyer's loyalty with $25 in rewards (in the form of a gift card) per $500 ordered.

Keep track in the CRM or spreadsheet and deliver the gift card in a thank you card once the threshold is reached to earn the gift card. Loyalty is royalty! The best fishing is when the fish are jumping into the boat (the catering buyer contacting the restaurant or placing a weekly or monthly standing order so the restaurant does not even have to "go fish").

Once you have all the targets identified and input into the CRM, it is time to start contacting those individuals. But what does one say? Email or phone call? Here comes the pitch.

The Pitch
Now that the potential buyers have been identified and targeted, it is time to contact the prospects on the list to pitch, "Why Buy Catering?" The pitch

PILLAR 3: *Sales*

can be done via email or phone. Create, review, and practice a 60-second catering pitch to communicate quality, value, and accuracy to the busy person on the other end of the phone. If calling, feel free to fill in the blanks on this template.

Call/Email Example 1

Hi, my name is _____. I am the manager/owner of the _____ restaurant in town, and we deliver the best _____ _____to feed your hungry group with our on-time team.

Call/Email Example 2

Hi, my name is _____ with _____, and we can fuel your team by serving the best sandwiches, salads, and more all while doing great things in our community. A portion of every sale supports the local community through our _____ program. We can make your catering simple and easy and make you look like the catering hero. What email can I send you the catering menu? Do you have any upcoming needs we can solidify right now?

Band Contact Example

Hi, my name is _____, and I'm a band parent. I understand the need to be on-time and have things clearly labeled. I would like to discuss our game day and competition meals as well as how we can help the band through fundraiser nights as we can help make more money than we can give.

Wow! Tons of actionable, practical effective steps to begin marketing and selling catering. Time to start fishing in the right places—with the right hooks and proper bait

Order Taking

We are ready to accept orders—but how? By using the main store phone number (which may not be answered properly, if at all)? Or the general email box checked once a day? Hardly a way to compete with the more sophisticated operators. Some companies even have professional third-party call centers that handle catering (i.e., the competition is fierce). In order to DOMINATE catering, the restaurant needs the following.

 *Catering Domination*

Dedicated Catering Phone Number

Commit to a standalone number for the leads and prospects to call. Google can provide a free number or obtain a toll-free number. Worse case, the owner's cell-phone, which is certainly not ideal, as callers may be ignored thinking it is a spam call.

Ensure whomever is answering the call is skilled and trained on order placement. "Frictionless" is the new term for guest service. Ensure it is simple (frictionless) to order. Avoid making it difficult for the guest to place the order—or he/she will place it elsewhere. Things to avoid include:

- Poor phone manners
- Putting guest on hold
- Asking guest to "call the catering manager"
- Ill-trained order-taker (versus a professional salesperson)

Remember, every time the catering phone rings, it is "MONEY" calling.

Dedicated Catering Email

Next, have a dedicated catering email starting with "catering@ ...". Look professional in the eyes of the buyer to start building trust (e.g., catering@smartrestaurantgroup.com). Keep the email simple and easy to remember. Forward the email to the dedicated person or people responsible for catering. Ensure the inquiries are replied to quickly (frictionless for guest). When a fisherman feels a nibble on the hook—boom! He instantly sets the hook and reels the fish in. Same with catering: The faster the response, the more catering can be closed.

Customer Relationship Manager (CRM)

Step three is the CRM. It is the power tool to ensure catering DOMINATION. As mentioned earlier, a spreadsheet can be used, but those who play in the big leagues of catering use a CRM to automate processes so the catering team can SELL catering and not be bogged down in administrative tasks. The main functionality (and benefits) of the CRM are as follows.

PILLAR 3: *Sales*

Manage Contacts
The CRM is the catering hub of information—names, emails, addresses, phone numbers, industry segment, events, birthdays, and so on. Without this valuable tool, one will spend far too much time on tracking the information, or, like most restaurants, they simply will not do anything with the information, lose sales, and blame others.

Activity Reports
Another valuable function the CRM performs is activity reports. The system can be where the lead came from and track order history. The CRM will set reminders to follow up via email or phone. It can be programmed to send thank you cards to large orders or first-time clients. The system can also generate reports based on sales and frequency—or infrequency of orders such as guests who have not ordered in 30, 60, or 90 days. Who are your top-10 catering clients? The CRM knows. Send the top-10 list a thank you. Look at what percentage of the total catering sales are generated by the top-10 (or 20) clients. Treat those who perform well for you like platinum-level frequent fliers. Reward and recognize their loyalty and ensure they feel special.

Promote Growth
The CRM system enables sales, marketing, and operations to work together and promote business growth. For instance, if multiple people are working on the catering business, all can have access to the data. Sales and marketing can use the leads to target highly profitable prospects, segment customers to market more effectively, and incentivized lapsed users. The operations team will utilize the calendar and production reports to ensure the team is prepared. Leadership has access to product mix data to see the most frequently ordered items and pricing. This information allows strategic decision-making to build sales and raise profitability. Teamwork.

Administrative Time Reduction
The CRM stores details, triggers, reminders, and activities. Automated

tasks can be programmed to send out reminder letters or emails to CPAs before tax season, football coaches and band directors in July, retailers in early October (for Black Friday), and so on. To maximize its effectiveness, information must be maintained, entered, and updated. It also requires the removal of old, duplicate, or obsolete entries.

Ready to dominate? At this point, prioritize the marketing and sales efforts. Start small with the lowest-hanging fruit around the restaurant. Start stacking wins (getting orders), generating a return on investment, and gearing up operations.

CHAPTER ACTION ITEMS

> Obtain dedicated phone number

> Setup dedicated email (forward to appropriate person/people)

> Implement fishbowl in-store

> Setup spreadsheet or CRM

> Prioritize list-building groups (i.e., schools, churches, pharma reps, etc.)

> Develop pitch emails and call scripts

> Begin pitching!

> Update CRM/spreadsheet with contacts

PILLAR 4
Operations

"Don't bother telling the world you are ready. Show it. Do it."
—Peter Dinklage

Sales and marketing can generate all the catering in the world, but if operations cannot execute the orders, not only is money wasted on the marketing efforts, guests are lost for life. Catering guests, rightfully so, have high expectations. The order total is quite high (usually over $150), so expectations are far higher than a guest visiting the restaurant and ordering a $6–$20 meal. After all, whoever selected the restaurant puts his/her reputation on the line, and that person is trusting the restaurant to perform flawlessly.

The most effective operators have systems in place to ensure consistent execution regardless of who the manager is or which team members are working. As an operator, solid, proven systems for catering must be in place along with well-trained team members. The key system areas needed are:

- Communication
- Training
- Prep
- Production
- Delivery and Setup

As mentioned earlier, catering is a different business. While some restaurants take reservations or have groups or parties booked in advance, most restaurants wait for guests to walk in, place online orders, or drive-through and then make their food. Catering, however, is radically different. Some guests order days in advance; others at the last minute. Some book through third-party websites; others call, fax, or email orders in, and some

 Catering Domination

place them online. Some need delivery; others pick up the order. What's a manager to do? Relax. Systems are the answer.

The good news? Often times, the catering order is placed with plenty of notice, resulting in time to prep and produce around normal business. The downside? Sometimes orders arrive with a short lead time, at the worst possible time with everything else going on, and, undoubtedly, the day the shift was understaffed or ill-prepared. While every issue cannot be eliminated, systems ensure the team is ready for the bulk of catering orders thrown at the restaurant. Let's start with communication.

Communication

Keeping the entire team updated is paramount to catering success and ensuring each team member knows his/her role. Whether the order is booked in-store, online, over the phone, or through a third-party app, most likely the entire staff (or those directly involved) needs to be aware of the upcoming orders, so prep and execution can be flawless.

Communication Tools

If the restaurant is using catering software, much of the communication cadence and systems are built into the software. If no catering software is utilized, it is up to the managers (or catering manager/salesperson if there is one) to ensure all necessary personnel are in the loop regarding catering. Group text apps or staff communication apps with links to calendars and pop-up text notifications are a great tool for those who want catering domination, as the app keeps everyone who needs to know "in the know".

Calendar

Whether the software calendar is used or Google Calendar, a spreadsheet or handwritten, ensure the following:

- All catering orders are entered into the calendar. Program alerts into the calendar with reminders one day in advance to do the necessary prep and the morning of the order for production reminders. Update the calendar as needed with new orders or changes to existing orders.

PILLAR 4: *Operations*

Use technology to ensure no mistakes or the "didn't know we had a catering order today" excuse.
• Ensure key personnel has access to view the calendar via app or computer. Text or send alerts for short-notice orders and/or changes. Everyone needs to talk the same lingo—keep it concise and clear and request confirmation.

Order Form

For guests who call orders in (or place via email), have a system to take the orders and gather all necessary information. Again, if using catering software, these features are typically built-in. If not using a CRM, ensure the restaurant has a standard order form. Everyone who takes orders can obtain the necessary information from the guest as well as provide consistent information and answer any questions from the caller. The order form should contain:

- Order details including special requests and any dietary restrictions
- Pickup time or delivery time, location address, and specific directions for the setup (and contact person on-site if not the caller)
- Contact name, phone number, and email
- How payment is being made

Other Forms

The following forms are recommended if the restaurant does not have catering software that automatically provides this information:

- **Ordering form:** Calculates quantity of each item to be added to food distributor (or applicable vendor) order when the catering order is known well in advance.
- **Prep form:** Quantity of each item to prep. NOTE: This form might need to be set up by day for prep (i.e., two days prior complete—; one day prior complete—; day of complete—).
- **Production form:** Calculates quantity of each item to produce for the order. This form is used the day of order production to ensure all items are completed.
- **Labels:** Printing labels versus handwriting on the items in the order or boxed lunches provides a much more professional look for the

 Catering Domination

guest. Labels should be printed in advance for any item in the order requiring information such as a person's name or being labeled for guests to know what is in their order.

- **Packing list:** To ensure zero mistakes and 100% accuracy, print a packing list of all items required in the order, especially frequently missed items (condiments, utensils, plates, cups, sides, bags of ice). When the guest arrives to pick up the order or prior to the driver leaving for the delivery, this checklist ensures all items are with the order. The guest will appreciate it.
- **Delivery driver setup checklist:** To ensure stellar service on-site, provide the delivery driver (even if it is a third-party driver) with the catering setup standards checklist. Guests have high expectations and often pay a premium for catering; their experience needs to exceed their expectations. Ensure the driver sets up the catering and sends the photo of the setup to the home office to ensure we can share with others.

Training

Once the communication process is in place and being utilized, it's time to train the team members. Review how to make each catering item and utilize all the forms. Allow them to sample the more unique catering items, so that every team member can explain the catering menu and options with the manager.

If training materials are not currently available, take digital photos of prep, step-by-step order assembly, and packaging, so the team member can see our catering standards. Train to those standards. Ensure all team members working on catering are aware of recipes and specs and how to prepare each item on the catering menu. When training production of catering orders, any leftover training food can be donated to local offices/stores (they can be the "Business of the Day" winner) who may be looking down the road for a caterer.

Prep & Production Charts

The day prior to any large catering orders, ensure the production and prep chart information has been entered. Print out the production and prep

PILLAR 4: *Operations*

charts or enter the information into the spreadsheet, so it can be calculated. Once the prep charge is printed, review the list, prep, and properly store any item to help get ready for the order the following day.

Last minute order? Take the order. Especially if using a third-party site, the restaurant is penalized if orders are declined. That moves the location down the list and makes it harder for future guests to find the restaurant. If taking a last-minute order, don't overload the basic operations of the restaurant; ensure any prep is completed in a timely fashion and/or prep to replace what was used for the catering order.

Once the prep chart is being used—and the staff needs to know WHY—move on to the forms needed the day of the delivery:

- **Production chart:** Shares how much of each item to make for the order.
- **Packing list:** Ensures all sides, special orders, condiments, utensils, plates, and napkins are included
- **Driver checklist:** Ensures all items are supposed to be in the bag to be delivered.

Each form is filled out for each order, so managers can easily check if the order is 100% right and ready on time.

Prep

Use the prep chart the DAY BEFORE the order. The team member or manager completes the prep chart and finishes prepping each item. It may be as simple as slicing meats for sandwiches, prepping extra meat for the fajita or burger bar, or setting up items the team will need the following day to actually produce the order such as assembling boxed lunches.

Additionally, if there is a large amount of catering scheduled the following day, a sound operational practice is to finish extra prep for the next day (for regular menu items), so there is less strain on the opening team, since they will have so much catering to prepare. Help team members deliver a flawless guest experience by thinking (and prepping) ahead.

 *Catering Domination*

Production Chart/Recipe Cards

Use the production chart (or recipe cards) to make the catering order. Ensure cold items are stored with cold items and hot with hot. Items that are prone to leak, such as dressings or sauces, must be tightly sealed and wrapped in plastic to prevent spills. Store the order in the proper staging area, cooler, or hot box.

Packing List

Use the packing list to ensure all items are in with the order and packed properly. The list should include EVERYTHING needed for the order, including cutlery kits, cups, side items, sauces, bags of ice, ice scoop/bucket, napkins, plates, and so on: 100% accuracy on 100% of the orders. If the order is prepared in advance and stored, it is critical that orders with items in various locations (i.e., cold sandwich tray in cooler and hot soup in warming cabinet) be labeled clearly and noted on this form, so nothing is missed when the guest is picking up or order is being delivered. Double-check the packing list with the guest for pickup orders or with the driver before he/she departs, so the delivery is flawless.

Delivery & Set Up

Schedule a driver for the delivery or have a third-party delivery company set up to do the delivery with minimal operations disruption. Deliveries CANNOT be late—insure the driver leaves in plenty of time to safely arrive at the destination.

Operations are the backbone of the restaurant. Catering is often a love/hate relationship with operations. When business is slow, everyone wants the restaurant to receive catering orders. When it is moderately busy, far too often the phone goes unanswered, and a potential catering client now calls the competitor. It can test operations' will and fortitude at times, while other times management is rejoicing over the huge catering sales and profit improvement. Balancing both as a leader is the key to success. Either way, operations are the lever to catering domination.

PILLAR 4: Operations

CHAPTER ACTION ITEMS

➤ *Calendar setup and implemented*

➤ *Training conducted (phone, selling, prep, production)*

➤ *All forms/checklists created and/or modified and implemented: prep, production, labels, packing list, pickup checklist, delivery checklist*

PILLAR 5
Delivery & Pickup

"You need to let the little things that would ordinarily bore you suddenly thrill you."
—Andy Warhol

UNTIL THIS POINT IN THE CATERING JOURNEY, the restaurant has had little, if any, interaction with the guest. Unless the order was called in, there has been no verbal interaction with the guest. All the work has been focused on the product: ensuring the order is prepared properly, accurately, and timely. Accuracy does not just mean "everything is in the bag". Accuracy must exist in all areas: quality (accurate) of the meal, all items included with the order (sides, utensils, condiments, plateware), and in the service interaction. Accuracy builds trust. Finally, all the hard work has come to fruition, as the food is about to be provided to the guest—or at least a delivery company taking the order to the guest.

As with the other pillars, systems and standards are the keys to consistently top-notch execution. Catering expectations are high with the guest. He/she expects perfection—the guest's reputation is staked on how well the team performs making the order. There are three primary types of catering orders: pickup, drop-off, and full-service catering. Group ordering can also be pickup or drop-off. Though a group order may vary from traditional catering (i.e., ordered from the regular menu), the standards outlined here would still apply. Let's review each type of catering in more detail.

Pickup Catering

This type of catering is the simplest to execute, as the guest is coming to the restaurant to pick up his/her order. Key points of an effective pickup catering experience include the following.

PILLAR 5: *Delivery & Pickup*

Pre-Pickup

- Ensure packing list has been completed in advance of guest arrival and is 100% accurate.
- Package all hot items together and all cold items together. Common sense but not common practice in many places.
- Order paid? If so, have receipt available and ready for arriving guest. If not, ensure payment is collected when guest arrives.
- Order is staged in the proper area.
- If multiple bags or boxes with the order, each is labeled clearly (1 of 3, 2 of 3) and any part of the order stored remotely (soup is in warming cabinet, bag of ice in freezer, etc.); note where additional items for the order are on the packing list so the item is not missed.
- Include coupons in the bag (brand approved and if allowed) for each attendee. If the order says it is for 12 people, include 12 coupons.
- Text, email, or call the guest to let him/her the order is ready and where to pick it up (to-go area, curbside, at the bar, host stand, etc.).

Pickup: Inside

Ensure the host, bartender, or cashier is aware of any catering orders and has a list of the names. When the guest arrives, greet him/her enthusiastically. Great first impressions are made when the guest feels like the restaurant is expecting them. Confirm the guest's name and retrieve order or walk the guest to the designated pickup area. Double-check the order with the guest by physically checking every item (including utensils, plates, serving utensils, etc.) and showing the guest to ensure nothing is missed. Ask if he/she needs any additional condiments as well.

If payment needs to be collected, process at this time. Always use the guest's name and offer to carry the order out to the car. Thank the guest and let them know you will see them again for their next catering order.

Pickup: Curbside

Many restaurants offer curbside pickup to ensure a frictionless guest experience. If the restaurant offers this service, guests will either call when they arrive or have provided a description of their car so the restaurant will

 *Catering Domination*

know which order is for that guest.

Confirm if payment has already been made. If so, bring the receipt. If not, find out how the guest will be paying and process the payment. Deliver the food to the car, review the contents of the order to ensure 100% accuracy, and thank the guest for his/her business.

Drop-Off Catering

Ideally, the restaurant's employees would be the ones interacting with the catering guests by making deliveries. However, more and more operators rely on third-party delivery companies to make the catering deliveries. Many perform at a high level and ease operational headaches for the restaurant by allowing them to focus on food while the third-party company makes the delivery.

If a third-party delivery company is used, the restaurant loses some control over the delivery experience and needs to ensure the delivery companies they choose to work with ensure high standards are executed as the delivery company is an extension of the restaurant in the eyes of the catering guest.

Pre-Delivery

Prior to the delivery leaving the restaurant, ensure the following items are in place. Many restaurants get lazy, as they deliver a higher volume of catering, so avoid slacking. While the restaurant may be doing dozens of catering orders, the guest only cares about his/her order. No excuses! Only 100% accurate, on-time deliveries. As Wyatt Earp said, "Fast is fine, but accuracy is everything. Take your time in a hurry." Keys to being ready on-time and accurately:

- Ensure packing list has been completed in advance of driver leaving and is 100% accurate. Ensure all items are with the order such as cutlery kits, serving utensils, branded/colored tablecloth, and ice bucket (if needed).
- Order paid? If so, have receipt stapled to bag. If not, ensure payment is collected at delivery.
- Know in advance if setup on-site is required or if the order is being dropped off at a reception area. Have the specific contact person and number for the driver.

PILLAR 5: *Delivery & Pickup*

- Order is staged in the proper area.
- If multiple bags/boxes, each is labeled clearly (1 of 3, 2 of 3, 3 of 3) and any part of the order stored remotely (soup is in warming cabinet; bag of ice in freezer, etc.); note on the packing list so it is not missed.
- Include coupons in the bag for each attendee. If the order says it is for 12 people, include 12 coupons.
- Text/email/call guest to let him/her know driver is on the way (and estimated time of arrival).
- Directions programmed into the phone GPS, so driver does not get lost or arrive late.

Delivery

Finally. Time to meet the guest and let the catering (and service) shine. The friendliness and helpfulness of the driver goes a long way in determining if future orders will be secured, so ensure the only focus is on making the guest/client happy by presenting an outstanding catering setup. Key points of an effective delivery catering experience include the following:

- A good habit is to text the contact letting the person know the order is on the way. Build trust.
- Be on-time (a few minutes early) and make contact with the guest/client upon arrival.
- No setup (just a drop-off)? Confirm all items in the order with the representative and process payment (or provide receipt if pre-paid); if guest requested no paperwork on site (i.e., he/she is buying for a client or it was paid through a third-party), do not ask for payment or a tip.
- Setup required? Set up the catering in the designated area (typically, the guest or a representative will show where to set up). Be courteous and respectful of the area working in. If unsure where to place items, ask the representative.
- Remove trash or packaging supplies.
- Take a photo of the setup once done and send to the restaurant. If the client who ordered the catering is not present, send the photo to that person as well. Build trust.
- When departing the building, take a photo of the building directory as well as any signage listing tenants in the neighboring buildings. Also,

 Catering Domination

note where any competitors' cars are delivering along the route to and from the restaurant. Why? Marketing. Potential clients to be contacted. Pass the company names to the person responsible for catering marketing (or start contacting them).

Full-Service Catering

As mentioned earlier, this book is focused on pickup and delivery catering versus full-service catering. Again, please refer to resources on full-service catering, as the service levels are far more involved. Here are a few key basics when providing full-service catering:

- Confirm arrival time and setup area in advance with the client
- All food/beverage/paper/utensils/serving utensils ready in advance
- Third-party vendors (party rental company, music, bar service, etc.) contacted and aligned on timing and responsibilities
- Head staff member briefed on client, event details, service level desired, event flow, etc.
- Driver and staffing routed with directions, setup plan, and service flow for the event
- Arrive, check in with the on-site contact, set up, and check all products
- Take photos of setup
- Discuss any specific needs with the host
- Provide outstanding service for the event

Follow-up after the order will be covered in the next chapter. Studies have shown a direct correlation between employee friendliness and intent to return/reorder as well as intent to recommend. Quality food and packaging along with 100% accuracy earn good reviews. Adding a stellar delivery and follow-up experience ensures high probability the guest orders from the restaurant the next time he/she has a catering need.

Competition in the catering arena is tough, and many competitors are quite sophisticated. Incorporating these proven ideas and tactics can be the difference-maker to set the brand apart and be the catering choice of many in the area. Do not be just one of the choices. Be thought of as the *only* one who does what you do. That's catering domination.

PILLAR 5: *Delivery & Pickup*

CHAPTER ACTION ITEMS

➤ *Pickup procedures standardized, trained, and implemented*

➤ *Curbside procedures standardized, trained, and implemented*

➤ *Delivery procedures standardized, trained, and implemented*

➤ *If offering full-service catering: procedures standardized, trained, and implemented*

PILLAR 6
Follow-Up

"Either you follow-up or you fold-up."
—Bernard Kelvin Clive

ONCE THE FOOD HAS BEEN DELIVERED, it is natural to think the job is finished. However, a few minor but important details still remain. As briefly mentioned in the previous chapter, follow-up is rarely done by the catering competition and can help the brand stand out. People buy from those they trust. Effective follow-up builds trust. The follow-up keys include:

- Order follow-up
- CRM updated
- Debrief with the team
- Thank you card mailed out (yes, thank you card, and yes, mailed)

Order Follow-Up (Day of Order)

Approximately two to four hours after the order has been picked up or delivered, call, text, or email the guest to ensure the order was to his/her liking and ask if there were any issues. Some catering software has an autogenerated follow-up email or text feature. If the system does not generate it automatically or a manual spreadsheet is being used, send the text or email. While the call may go to voice mail or no reply is received from the email or text, do not worry or get offended. Following up, even if no response from the guest, accomplishes the following:

1) It shows the guest the restaurant is genuinely concerned about the catering experience. Most competitors do not do this critical step; however, it helps the restaurant stand out and proves the commitment to excellence.

2) It gives a chance to inquire about booking the next event.

PILLAR 6: *Follow-Up*

3) It helps uncover minor issues that likely never would have been mentioned. Too often, guests simply accept mediocrity and then either say nothing (and never order from us again) or trash the restaurant on social media. Following up in this fashion generates feedback from the guest and allows the team to work on improvements based on the guest's input.

4) If there is a problem, the guest is aware the restaurant cares based on being contacted, and it allows an opportunity to fix the issue.

5) Encourage the guest to post a review on social media sites or the third-party site he/she ordered from. Potential catering buyers look at reviews on social media sites as "trusted" sources, so remind the catering guest to post a review, as it can help generate future orders from other catering guests.

If the order was a first-time guest, or the order was large, call the guest. Thank the guest for the order and for trusting the restaurant to help make it amazing. Perhaps a surprise perk is added to the loyalty account for the guest or a token of appreciation is mailed or emailed to them. Make the guest say "Wow!"

The more one stays in front of the guest in a nonpushy, nonsales way, the more top of mind the brand is when the guest wants to reorder. Go above and beyond. Do the little things, such as follow-up, that the competition does not do. Stand apart. Be the only name the guest needs to know for catering—that is catering domination.

CRM Updated

While sitting at the computer or on the phone following up with the guest, log in and update the CRM (or spreadsheet) with the order information such as order date, details of the order, and the total. If the system has an autogenerated email, text, or card feature, ensure it is activated for this order so the follow-up happens automatically. Double-check the CRM or spreadsheet to note upcoming events that might require catering.

Another way to build relationships is by inputting reminders into the CRM (or spreadsheet); for example, special occasions, prime catering times for

 Catering Domination

clients, or in advance of annual events. Examples could include upcoming Black Friday catering for retail clients, monthly or quarterly meetings for the company, or an anniversary or birthday. Do not be overbearing. Simply remind guests as a service to stay in contact and be top of mind when the guest is ready to place the next order.

Finally, review the monthly reports, as the CRM can provide frequency reports showing which guests have not ordered for a few weeks or months. If using a spreadsheet, sort the data by "last order date" to obtain similar information. Either way, contact those guests with a "We Miss You" message. Much of the competition is not taking these extra steps to connect with the catering guest, though some are. Do what the leaders and experts do.

Practice like the pros. Yes, it will be inconvenient until these behaviors become a habit. However, these habits make the brand memorable and top of mind, no different than the product or service the guest receives. Be memorable and dominate—or be forgotten.

Debrief with the Team

One valuable system the military uses (and restaurants should use in all areas) is the mission debrief. Once the mission is complete, the leaders meet to discuss what went right, what went wrong, and what needs to be done different (or improved) on the next mission. S.M.A.R.T. managers should already use a pre-shift and now add a post-shift debrief to improve performance. For catering orders, great managers debrief with the team once the order is complete.

- What went right?
- Were there any issues?
- What needs to be improved?

Unless the manager is 100% involved in the order-taking, production, and pickup or delivery process, he/she will be unaware of some of the details. Review with the team the three questions above. Take the feedback constructively and make necessary modifications to future orders. Perhaps someone forgot a vital piece of information when taking the order, the

PILLAR 6: *Follow-Up*

delivery instructions were unclear, or the restaurant was out of an item and someone had to scramble and buy it locally. The debrief is meant to remove obstacles for future orders and ensure the team continues to improve.

Thank You Cards

The old man sitting on the porch can complain all day long about how today's generation is lacking manners. He is probably correct, though today's generation often thinks a text "TY" is as sufficient as a thank you note. While one may think the text, email, or call follow-up is sufficient, where have all the thank you cards gone? Thank you cards (yes, real ones in the real mail) are a nice personal touch showing the client how important he/she is to the business.

Parents often have their children send handwritten thank you notes whenever a gift is received. How does it feel to receive a handwritten note as a thank you? Probably feels special, and the gesture will typically be remembered. Sadly, however, thank you notes have become a lost art in the world of text, email, and social media. The last impression makes a lasting impression. Do what others do not. Go above and beyond. What is the harm in being a bit more kind than the competitor? Oh, right, catering DOMINATION.

Why not take that act of kindness and apply it to the business? Most sales books preach to business owners to find additional touchpoints to engage and interact with customers. Want to have a school of fish (hungry catering buyers) swimming nearby that is easily scooped up in a net? It is far easier to keep existing catering clients than find new ones—and these are right here, right now.

Whether the manager or a team member with good handwriting writes the note, simply thank the guest for his/her support. This genuine note of appreciation not only serves as a nice gesture of follow-up but also a marketing opportunity. This simple act provides an additional point to market for their next order (catering coupon) or an offer to come to the restaurant.

Whether using a spreadsheet or a CRM, utilizing these four simple yet

 *Catering Domination*

powerful follow-up steps helps engage the guest, fosters the relationship, builds trust, and gets the brand closer to having a guest for life. Catering domination will result.

CHAPTER ACTION ITEMS

- Order follow-up procedures established and practiced
- Spreadsheet/CRM updated with each order
- Debrief with the team after each catering order/delivery
- Thank you card mailed out
- Large or first-time orders contacted personally by phone

PART 3

Action

CHAPTER 4
Fishing in a Barrel Tactics

"Your odds of success improve when you are forced to direct all of your energy and attention to fewer tasks."
—James Clear

THIS CHAPTER FOCUSES ON SPECIFIC TYPES of catering guests/clients and how to find, sell-to, and execute an effective catering program for the respective groups ... like fishing in a barrel. These tactics have worked well for restaurants, so don't reinvent the wheel. Fish in the barrel!

Guests

Every guest is an opportunity. Before fishing in other barrels, fish inside the restaurant (today's guests). See beyond the transaction. Get to know the guest. Where does he/she work? What activities or groups are they or their family involved in? Learn to better serve guests' catering needs once aware of the potential sales opportunity those guests have.

As mentioned previously, always be connecting dots (ABCD). Use the clues. Guest in a company-logoed hat, jacket, or shirt? Ask about catering. Guest wearing company or school lanyard? Ask about catering. Guest wearing name badge or paying with a company credit card? Ask about catering. Guest wearing football, band, or other school group/team paraphernalia? Ask about catering.

One will be amazed how much catering business can be earned simply by talking to guests. Many are unaware that catering is available or are not thinking about the brand when they need to order catering. Ensure that knowledge, and the brand, is top of mind when the guest needs to place that next catering order.

FISHING IN A BARREL TACTICS

Schools

When building the targeted contact list for these types of groups, it is fishing for HUGE fish in VERY small barrels. Teacher orders can range from 15–200 boxed meals depending on the size of the school. Team meals can vary from 10–150, depending on the sport, for multiple games over the course of a season. High school bands are often 150–300+ members plus support staff.

NOTE: Schools/school districts often have a strict vendor approval process, so comply. If the school or district is paying the restaurant directly, the restaurant must be an approved vendor. If it is the booster club or teachers paying with their own money, typically the restaurant does not have to be on the approved list, but it certainly helps when letting the school/groups know the restaurant is already approved.

In many areas, middle-school sports and groups are also an option. Promoting the team meals as a pre-game meal can create a niche perhaps not currently available. When we first started our team meal deals, many middle schools were not even doing pre-game meals. We created the market by providing the service to the parents, presenting at the pre-season parent meeting and doing all the work, so the coach only had to worry about coaching. Sometimes when a potential client says "no", a bit more work simply needs to be done to guide the guest to "yes". Time to go fish.

Teacher In-Service/Testing Days

Offering a discounted boxed lunch on in-service or testing days not only builds sales, it also builds goodwill. Support the teachers and schools, and it will be paid back in droves (always try to support donation request as well such as gift cards/coupons for teacher appreciation or holiday season). Arrange the lunch with the admin or school secretary, perhaps with a 20% discount as a "nice to do". Typically, teachers are using their own funds, so it's a nice thing to provide a discount (as is recommended for fire/EMT/police). Provide an order form or online link for the group to place its order. When delivering, include coupons that are good for purchase online or in-store—and promote ongoing group orders, as the restaurant could easily

 *Catering Domination*

do groups of six or more boxed lunches (if not too far) on a regular basis.

Team/Group Meals

Teams are a HUGE opportunity for any restaurant offering a boxed meal of a sandwich/entrée, chips, and a cookie or dessert. As mentioned earlier, our group builds an entire business around schools. Contact the booster club and coach for the high school teams and the coach for college and middle schools. It has to be TIMELY. For high school football, contact them before the Fourth of July, as the seasons start in early August in many areas. For other sports or groups/clubs, contact them about four to six weeks prior to their need and follow-up as the date gets closer if the deal is not yet solidified.

It is recommended to give back to the programs that support the restaurant through sponsorships or food donations to the press box or coaches' meetings as a gesture of thanks for the business—and it can be huge business. Most restaurant managers or owners have been hit up for an ad in the program or sign on the field or other types of donation requests. To make it mutually beneficial for all (MBA), let the booster rep or coach know a small donation or sponsorship can be made, but a larger donation can be made in return for being the exclusive meal provider for the team.

To illustrate, let the team/group know, "We can donate $100 to the team, or we could donate $500 if we are the exclusive meal provider to the team for the season." MBA! A high school football team may have 50–70 players on varsity, 50–70 on sub-varsity, and another 70–100 on the ninth-grade team. Playing 10 games per season x 250 meals per week x $7/box nets over $17,500 in sales. All that for a $500 investment? No brainer. Imagine a guaranteed $1,750 per week for 10 weeks. Big business. Suggestions/perks to help seal the deal:

- Order online option
- Order full season or partial season package (versus game by game)
- Free delivery—a must!
- Donate bottled water. Warehouse stores sell it for 7–8 cents per bottle,

FISHING IN A BARREL TACTICS

a small price to pay to earn big orders. Worse case, add it as an option for $.50/meal.
- One coach meal free for every 10 boxed meals ordered—inexpensive way to earn big orders
- Customization of the sandwich/entrée. Being in the sandwich business, with 100% certainty, this option earned us more business than any other tactic. All competitors simply do ham or turkey. Offering six to eight different options and some customization seals the deal. If not a sandwich place, no problem. Simply offer three to five choices and let the athletes rotate choices halfway through the season to avoid burnout.

In regards to ordering online, sites such as Wufoo and Google Docs have payment interfaces with groups like Square, so the restaurant can set up a customized online ordering page for each team or group. Set up a package for the number of meals for the season (i.e., five or ten games or however many the team needs). Then, send out the link to the booster club to forward to the parents and the orders are sent to the manager. SIMPLE. Parents love this system (easy to order and pay for entire season) as do coaches who do not want to handle the funds. Orders come right to the store and are saved to use for the season.

Contests/Events (theater, band, drum line, cheer, drill team, track, swim)

Remember the 4,400 boxed lunch orders for a band contest mentioned in the introduction? Band contests often have 15–40 bands comprised of 150–300+ members each who need TWO meals on contest day. That's over 2,000 potential boxed lunches (or dinner meals served) on one day. Historically, these contests start in late September and end in early November, so start fishing in late July/early August.

Track meets, debate contests, cheer, drill team, or drumline competitions all have dozens of schools, albeit with much fewer members than band, in one location all day in need of catering being delivered to the event. Look at the school and athletic calendars or contact the coaches or directors.

SMART RESTAURANT GUIDE TO Catering Domination

Have hooks in the water to catch the fish wanted. Get ready to fish for band contests:

- Search "HS marching band contests" (or track meets, swim meets, debate contests, etc.)?
- Find the contests/events in the area. Many have their own website, while others have consolidated contest lists all in one place (as an example, Bands of America hosts contests around the country and can be found at www.musicforall.org).
- If there is a list of the incoming teams/groups, search for their director/coach online (e.g., "Smith HS band director") to obtain their email. Add it to the spreadsheet or database.
- If there is NOT a list of the incoming teams/groups, find the event coordinator contact information on the site. See below for the second example of how to word that contact email.
- Contact the respective group or person similar to the below examples.

Incoming Band/Team/Group

"Good luck on the upcoming contest. I understand competition season and the resources it takes. Let us help with the food, so it's one less thing to worry about at the competition."

(This Part Would Be Customized to Your Brand)

"Kids get sick of ham or turkey sandwiches, and, since that's what most of our competition offers, we offer more: chicken pesto, ham, turkey, roast beef, buffalo chicken, club, Italian grinder, and an array of vegetarian options. We also offer salads or lettuce wraps for gluten-free needs."

"Each boxed meal is $7 and includes a 7-inch sandwich or salad, chips, and cookies (apples for G-F boxed meals). Free delivery. Contact me ASAP to reserve your meal slot as the slots fill up quickly. Thanks."

Contest/Event Host

"As a former band dad who has also fed tens of thousands of band kids at competitions around the state, we can add value to the bands attending the competition."

"I'd like to discuss promoting (my restaurant) as the preferred meal provider to the incoming bands; in turn, we will donate back to the program $1/box ordered. We offer far more choices than 'ham or turkey'

FISHING IN A BARREL TACTICS

and can guarantee we are 100% right and right on-time. Let me know a good time to discuss so we can provide recommended verbiage to send to the directors."

A similar approach can be taken for all types of other events, contests, and meets. Modify the relevant parts of the contact email for the event. Soon there will be HUGE fish in a small barrel.

Lunch-N-Learn

One of the quickest ways to ramp up catering sales is existing catering buyers. Have a client who works in a large company or office? Talk to that person about setting up a "lunch-n-learn" for all the catering buyers in the building/company. Provide a free lunch of catering offerings in return for a short presentation to the group on what can be provided. Great way to gather a large group of potential clients as the restaurant recommended already by one of the group.

Pharma Reps

Pharmaceutical reps, though hard to find, are a potential goldmine for catering, as they place orders for multiple doctor and medical offices. Taking care of the rep and his/her clients while ordering and delivering was covered earlier in the book. The recommended approach to finding pharma reps is:

- **LinkedIn:** Search for pharma reps in the area.
- **Medical offices:** Visit local medical offices and drop off samples or catering information. Ask the admins to pass along restaurant contact information to the pharma reps. Every pharma rep referred equals a free lunch for the admin.
- **Ambulance chasing:** Stake out large medical complexes before lunch. Bump into the reps in the lobby and provide a slick one-page pharma rep program with contact information included.

Pharma reps take work to find but are a key cog in the catering domination wheel.

 *Catering Domination*

Churches

While churches may have limited budgets, many still have a catering need for small meetings, group discussions, or large church events. Make the decision if the restaurant can be in their price range. Worst case, the restaurant generates an incredible amount of goodwill and brand awareness by providing catering, whether full price, discounted, or donated. Never forget the value of brand awareness and supporting those in close proximity. Reciprocate by providing Vacation Bible School (VBS) coupons during the summer or donating items when the church is volunteering in the local community. Contact the youth pastor/minister, office administrator, or event coordinator.

Car Dealers

Most car dealers tend to feed their sales and service staff on Saturday and also have a limited budget. Want the business? Sixty boxed lunches at $6/box is still $360 in sales and about $150–$180 in profit you will not have if the order is declined. Our group found a less-expensive cookie and smaller bag of chips to use in the discounted boxed lunches. Some places use a brown paper bag versus a box to save a few more cents. Ensure the quality of the brand is upheld. Saving 40 to 50 cents per boxed meal (while still providing great value) adds up to additional bottom-line savings and is another reason to say "yes" to the order.

Retail

Retailers' employees near the location are likely existing guests in many cases, especially for fast-casual and quick-service restaurants near their store. Retailers often have catering needs throughout the year. Well-known needs include Black Friday and the holiday shopping time. They also need catering for meetings, product launches, inventory, doing volunteer projects in the community, or on major sales days when the employees cannot leave for food. How does one find out who to talk to?

- Use the clues. If these employees are already eating in the restaurant, ask them who decides the catering choices for the store.

FISHING IN A BARREL TACTICS

- Perk the store with coupons for their employees.
- Drop off a catering tray.
- Contact the HR or store manager (arrive bearing food and coupons).

Real Estate Agents

Real estate agents often host open houses or provide food on move-in day for their clients. Agents can easily be met through the chamber of commerce. Remember "use the clues". Real estate signs are everywhere and contain their contact information—add them to your database. Obtain the contact information from the sign (or when meeting at a chamber meeting) and contact the agents regarding their catering needs.

Another option is to contact the various real estate agent offices (easily found via an online search) and do a lunch-n-learn at their next training meeting or workshop and introduce the services provided. Real estate agents (especially successful ones) are always part of the chamber. Hunting for new clients and referrals. Catering DOMINATION.

Funeral Homes

While uncomfortable to imagine, funeral homes have catering needs for their clients and families. Search online for the funeral homes in the area, send over a catering tray, or contact the director to discuss the catering needs. Visit mid-day, as this is the best opportunity to discuss catering services with the director. During this time of grief, the referral wants to ensure the attendees have food without any hassle. For that reason, there seems to be less price-sensitivity. Having a selection of trusted caters is important, and it is an incremental opportunity for the restaurant.

As with fishing, one must fish when the fish are biting. Car dealers decide on Wednesday or Thursday who will be providing their meals that week. Retailers are selecting Black Friday and holiday catering vendors in late September or early October. High school football and band often select providers by late July, so have those hooks in the water with the right bait and catch those fish.

 *Catering Domination*

> CHAPTER ACTION ITEMS
>
> ➤ *Conduct trade area analysis to determine "big fish" (i.e., largest catering potential clients)*
>
> ➤ *Prioritize targeted groups by size (potential) and seasonality (i.e., contact retail for Black Friday catering in late September or early October; football coaches and band in July, etc.)*
>
> ➤ *Assign various targeted groups to team members to enlist more help on building sales quickly*

CHAPTER 5
Action Plan & Implementation

"In order to kick ass you must first lift up your foot."
—Mel Robbins

TIME TO CHART A COURSE OF ACTION. Terminology should now be understood. Pillars in place to create a solid structure for catering domination. What next? Talking or reading about catering is simple. Making a difference and impact is a challenge—one now ready to be undertaken. Time to put the thoughts into action and create the implementation plan.

Let's start with where the restaurant is today.

Current

Average Catering Sales $/week	_____
Catering Sales YTD %	_____
Target Catering Sales $/week	_____

Competitors	

 Catering Domination

Catering Menu vs. Competition *(keep representative of the brand)*	

Current Catering Marketing	

Current Guest/Email Database of Catering Clients	

ACTION PLAN & IMPLEMENTATION

Action Plan

It's time to identify priorities and create a budget to grow catering sales. First and foremost, ensure the catering menu is competitive. If working for a chain, use the menu provided (but perhaps suggest updates to the home office if needed). Third, train the staff on all catering prep and production if not already done. Fourth, create a basic spreadsheet setup to track guests and their purchases (as well as marketing effectiveness). List out the ideal targets such as retail, schools, local offices, hospitals, etc. Make it a top-20 list and get after it. Start with the top-20 targeted businesses. Use low-hanging fruit and go after larger clients.

Initial Marketing Plan

Create a 90-day budget with marketing plan and prioritize high-return/low-cost methods of marketing first to build momentum and cash flow. This initial step should include:

- Fishbowl
- Email blasts to existing guests
- Training staff to identify potential catering guests in-store
- List building and feet-on-the-street for nearby businesses, office parks, churches, schools
- LinkedIn search for pharma reps in the area
- Claim or update the Google Business Page, Facebook (for catering), and social promotion of catering

Once the orders (and cash) start rolling in, it is time to work on the next wave of marketing methods, obtaining catering software (which have cost requirements), and ramping up the catering sales to another level, including:

- CRM setup and all data input
- Purchase lists of "look-alike buyers" (lists of companies similar to those who already buy catering from the restaurant)
- Click funnel setup and promoted via digital ads
- Seasonal reminders for respective types of buyers (i.e., retailers in early October, car dealers, school coaches, band directors, etc.)

SMART RESTAURANT GUIDE TO *Catering Domination*

Below is a sample weekly budget to help frame what a solid, inexpensive (but effective) plan would look like—and how much can be done with minimal investment. Some of these items may be printed in bulk to keep costs down. For illustration purposes, we spread the cost out per week; the coupons cost $90 to print and ship but it's done over a six-week time period expensed at $15/week.

Sample Weekly Budget

$20—*Fishbowl winner per week (one tray, dessert sampler)*

$20—*Business of the week feet-on-the-street giveaway (one tray, dessert sampler)*

$15—*Coupons for local businesses' employees while doing feet-on-the-street*

$20—*List cost plus direct mail post card cost (average the cost out per week)*

$30—*Labor for feet-on-the-street (2.5 hours per week x $12/hour)*

Initial Action Steps

Add detail to the steps above on the 90-day marketing plan. Put deadlines in place and stay the course. Similar to working out, nothing is noticed after a day or two, but one certainly feels uncomfortable in this new routine. Stay with it.

- Spreadsheet built and ready for new entries; existing clients'/guests' names added (one week).
- Get fishbowl with printed slips of paper to collect guest data (two weeks).
- Review potential third-party catering/delivery partners and sign up as needed (one week).
- Employee incentive put in place: 10% commission paid to person who brings in catering from existing dine-in guest or who secures order outside the restaurant through feet-on-the-street efforts or personal contacts (four weeks).
- If schools are a target, search online to build database of these positions: Principal, principal's administrative assistant, all coaches,

ACTION PLAN & IMPLEMENTATION

and group leaders to contact (theater, band, choir, drama, cheer, drill team, etc.); contact seasonally the respective coaches; know in-service and testing days to offer teacher meals by contacting admin/campus secretary in advance (four weeks).

- Coupons, postcards, and thank you cards printed (may print larger quantity to drive cost down and then use over time); determine areas to create cadence of marketing versus mailing all at one time (two weeks).
- Map out the area around the restaurant into zones or segment by business type (retail, medical, car dealers, schools, etc.) and create feet-on-the-street plan (two weeks).
- Train feet-on-the-street ambassadors and determine hours per week to the task (one to three days per week, midmorning or midafternoon), provide samples, catering info and coupons (two weeks).
- Train staff on catering prep and production, if needed; photos of catering setup to use for social media (use the meals made for training for the business of the day winner) (two weeks).
- Start making money.

Next Steps

Once the orders start coming in, ensure all orders are prepared accurately and deliveries made timely. Post photos of catering setup to social media accounts and post in the restaurant if space available. Update the spreadsheet with new guests' information as collected (fishbowl, feet-on-the-street, in-store, lists).

- Domain name purchased and set up for click funnel
- Purchase lists of "look-alike buyers" (lists of companies similar to those who already buy catering from the restaurant)
- Digital ads created; account(s) setup for channels to be used (Facebook, Instagram, TikTok, etc.)
- CRM setup and all data input
- Seasonal reminders for respective types of buyers (i.e., retailers in early October, car dealers, school coaches, band directors)

Follow up with every guest via phone or email—and mail (yes, real mail)

 *Catering Domination*

a thank you card to the person who booked the order. Post reviews and testimonials.

Next, keep the database up to date with how much each guest has spent, adding new potential clients and contacting those who have not ordered for 30–60 days. Do not forget to perk the top-10 buyers, as those guests are generating the cash needed to fund the next wave of marketing and accelerate the rise to domination.

Finally, start exploring the use of catering software and more sophisticated marketing tactics as catering sales grow. Operationally, the software will free up managers' time (and yours) from calculations, data entry, and printing forms to being able to spend more time marketing the catering services. Look at joining the chamber of commerce, providing the member meeting free food (VERY targeted use time and money), and expanding the delivery area to reach more potential clients.

Visit us online at www.cateringdomination.com for more resources, webinars, and unlimited coaching.

BOOM! Mic drop.

Are you ready to join the world of
CATERING DOMINATION?

Good luck!